BETRAYAL OF TRUST

BETRAYAL OF TRUST

Sexual Abuse by Men who Work with Children
– *In their own words*

Matthew Colton and **Maurice Vanstone**

FREE ASSOCIATION BOOKS • LONDON

Published in 1996 by Free Association Books Limited
57 Warren Street, London W1P 5PA
and 70 Washington Square South, New York, NY 10012–1091

© Matthew Colton and Maurice Vanstone 1996

The right of Matthew Colton and Maurice Vanstone to be identified as the
authors of this work has been asserted by them in accordance with the
Copyright, Designs and Patents Act 1988.

ISBN 1 85343 356 X hardback

A CIP catalogue record for this book is available from the British Library.

Produced for Free Association Books Ltd by Chase Production Services.
Printed in the EC by J. W. Arrowsmith Ltd, Bristol.

CONTENTS

1 OVERVIEW

> I have lost everything. I have thrown it away. Not only have I betrayed myself, I feel that other people here have betrayed themselves too. I have betrayed others and also feel that I have betrayed my profession, which is perhaps even more.

The quote with which we open this book correctly identifies the fact that the betrayal involved in the sexual abuse of children has dimensions to it that include the survivor of that abuse, the abuser, and the personal, cultural and professional context of his life. It also illustrates the openness that we encountered in our interviews with the seven men who are the subjects of this book, and it adds credence to the view that if we are to protect vulnerable children then, amongst other things, we have to listen to those people who might exploit their vulnerability.

All of the men involved themselves voluntarily, gave permission for publication and expressed their desire to make a contribution to child protection. It is our hope that to some degree they will have achieved that aim by providing in-depth material which throws some light on the thinking and motivation behind abusive behaviour, and which can be studied by other researchers as well as practitioners and managers in the relevant fields. Moreover, by making this book possible they will also have made a contribution to future research, because the royalties from its sales will be used to fund that research. This book is, therefore, dedicated to those subjects who had the courage to talk and also to their victims, whose hurt is seen but whose voices are unheard.

Child Sexual Abuse

Unfortunately, the sexual abuse of children appears to be a relatively widespread phenomenon. The British sociologist Anthony

Giddens (1989) states that *sexual abuse* may be defined as the carrying out of sexual acts by adults with children below the age of consent (16 years in Britain). The term *incest* refers to sexual activity between close relatives or kin. Not all incest is sexual abuse. Sexual intercourse between brother and sister, for example, is incestuous but cannot be described as abuse. In sexual abuse the adult exploits the child for sexual purposes (Giddens, 1989).

Until recently it was generally believed that sexual acts between adults and children were rare owing to the strong taboos against such behaviour. However, over the past ten or twenty years it has become increasingly clear that child sexual abuse is fairly common-place and exists at all levels of society. A nationwide study in the United States found an increase of 600 per cent in reported cases of child sexual abuse between 1976 and 1982 (Finkelhor, 1984). In Britain, the number of children on NSPCC registers under child sexual abuse rose exponentially from 7 in 1977 to 527 by 1986 (Birchall, 1989). The rise in reported cases probably results from the increased attention that is being paid to the problem by social welfare agencies and the police. It is also evident that such statistics are likely to represent only the tip of the iceberg.

The rapid 'discovery' of child sexual abuse as a social problem began in the United States, but quickly became an international phenomenon (CIBA Foundation, 1984). The issue may have lain dormant for so long partly because the taboos against such activity meant that welfare workers and researchers avoided asking questions about it to parents and children. The women's movement was influential in initially raising public consciousness about child sexual abuse as part of a broader campaign aimed at tackling sexual harassment and exploitation (Giddens, 1989). A major role was played by writers who were themselves survivors of sexual abuse, such as the American feminist, Rush (1980), who viewed sexual abuse as part and parcel of gender power inequalities.

However, an examination of the history of childhood reveals that child abuse, including sexual abuse, is not a new phenomenon, nor is public and state concern about it. Corby (1993) contends that the history of child abuse from antiquity through to the Middle Ages, on to Victorian times and up to the present, serves to counter two commonly held beliefs: first, the idea that the further back one goes into history the worse the treatment of children was; second, that it is only in recent times that societies such as ours have taken steps to deal with the problem. On this view, child abuse has not so much been 'discovered' as 'rediscovered' of late, a process which began with the rediscovery of physical abuse in the 1970s and 1980s.

In Britain, this was fuelled by a series of highly publicised deaths of children at the hands of parental figures, which led to an onslaught of criticism directed at social work agencies for failing to offer adequate protection to the children concerned (Parton, 1985). Perhaps the most notable of such tragedies were the cases of Maria Colwell and Jasmine Beckford, in that the official inquiries that followed resulted in major changes in child protection policy and practice (Beckford, 1985; Colwell, 1974; Hendrick, 1994; Parton, 1991).

Concern about the sexual abuse of children had been gradually increasing since the late 1970s among medical practitioners, therapists and child protection workers. However, the subject did not attract the attention of the general public until newspaper articles and television programmes on the problem began to appear in the 1980s. The publicity surrounding events in Cleveland during the summer of 1987 was particularly influential in raising public consciousness about child sexual abuse. The media reported that an unusually large number of children had been removed from their parents and placed into care by social workers acting on the recommendation of two paediatricians who, using a newly developed physical test, had diagnosed that the majority of the children had been anally abused (La Fontaine, 1990). The local MP supported the distraught parents and raised the matter in Parliament. This led to the establishment of a public inquiry chaired by Lord Justice Butler-Sloss, whose report had a far-reaching impact on the work of child protection agencies and prompted changes in child care law in the form of provisions contained in the Children Act 1989 (Cleveland County Council, 1988; Corby, 1993; Hendrick, 1994).

Data and Methods

The Cleveland controversy concerned alleged intra-familial child sexual abuse. However, recent years have witnessed scandals about extra-familial sexual abuse. Among the most notorious and disturbing of such cases have been those involving abuse by adults entrusted to work directly with children. Yet this subject has so far attracted little interest from academic researchers. Whilst studies have been undertaken on the perpetrators of sexual abuse (Finkelhor et al., 1990; Waterhouse et al., 1994; Briggs, 1995; Howitt, 1995), none have focused specifically on those whose employment touches upon the physical, spiritual and educational well-being of children. This is surprising, given that these are the very people who, when they do sexually abuse, often attract dramatic and lurid

media attention and bring a focus to the inadequate levels of protection for children who, far from being protected by their special
status, are exposed to greater risk.

This book is an essential component of the beginnings of a
broader project which aims to fill a serious gap in the research on
child sexual abuse. In this first stage we have attempted to enhance
understanding of what might have led subjects to abuse children in
their trust, through their subjective reconstructions of their own life
experiences. Because we believe that research methods must be
appropriate to research objectives, and because we wished to construct grounded theory in new territory, we decided to use unstruc-
tured interviews informed by the long tradition of life story work
(Plummer, 1983).

However, we cannot make claim to a life story approach in its
fullest sense of involving the subject in extensive interviews over
prolonged periods; the constraints of time and our research objectives prescribed a modified version involving two, and in some
cases, three interviews, spanning between four and six hours of
recorded conversation.

Our aim was to be facilitators as opposed to questioners and to be
as unobtrusive as possible, thereby restricting our influence over the
shape and direction of the subjects' contributions. Life story work is,
however, intervention and although all of the subjects chose their
starting point, our prompts and questions will inevitably have had an
impact on their thinking and triggered memories in ways that will
have contributed to the stories which emerge. This will have occurred
at the level of non-verbal as well as verbal interaction, and will have
been encompassed within a framework of unexpressed constructions
of masculinity by both researcher and subject. Each interview is the
result of two men talking, and to an extent, therefore, influence
operates in ways which are difficult to identify.

It was essential for the purpose of this study that the men
involve themselves voluntarily and were as informed as possible
about the nature of the research. They were not offered money for
participating, but were offered the opportunity to make a positive
contribution to child protection. Despite their voluntary involvement, as researchers we were faced with a number of ethical problems which we needed to resolve in order to continue with the
study. Perhaps the most fundamental of these problems was
whether or not research of the kind we were undertaking was
exploitative, not only of the men themselves but of their many
victims. In our own discussions we were never able entirely to
persuade ourselves that the research was completely devoid of any

exploitative dimension. Exploitation is invariably for some gain, and for us the issue of moral justifiability rests on the nature of that gain. As we have indicated previously the research involves no material gain for us as researchers, although if the book is favourably received we may have gained in terms of reputation. However, the over-arching objective of this book and our broader research is to help protect children from future sexual abuse by professionals and this gain, if achieved, seems to be both ethical and moral.

We were faced also with the dilemma of how we could encourage the men to be as open as possible, without heightening their vulnerability. It has been essential, therefore, for us to work hard at fulfilling our promise of confidentiality and, to this end, factual detail that might be linked to both offender and victim has been either removed or altered. Accordingly, there has been a fictionalising of aspects of these stories, but we have been careful to ensure that their essential meanings and messages have been retained. Each of the men gave his written permission for us to publish the outcomes of the interviews, subject to the guarantee of confidentiality.

As the presenters of this book, we have contributed from our different perspectives, which in turn are drawn from our respective professional and life experiences. Our own life stories, therefore, although untold, have influenced the way that we approached the study. To the degree to which we can understand that influence, we can say that it emanates from a shared conviction that a child does not have the capacity to make informed choices about sexual involvement with an adult, and that such involvement is inevitably the result of abuse of power by the adult. However, we have had to consciously inhibit our natural reactions to some of the discourse of the men and to limit overt challenging of attitudes and distorted thinking in order to facilitate a process that enabled their stories to be told.

We make no claims for representativeness of this sample; it is obviously too small, and the data collected cannot be used to test theories about why people use work situations to abuse. That, however, was not our purpose. Rather, we were seeking to formulate grounded theory which would inform the focus not only of our future research but also that of others. All the men who were interviewed at the time of their offences were involved in the care of children through their work. We use the word 'care' in its broadest sense to include physical, psychological, and spiritual care as well as education. The offences committed against the children include rape, buggery and indecent assault. Those pruriently looking for details of those offences in this book will be disappointed.

Content and Structure

As indicated, our aim in the first stage of our research was to be as non-intrusive as possible and we have attempted to be consistent with this principle in the construction and presentation of this book. Our contribution is, first, to provide an introduction to existing knowledge on the sexual victimisation of children, which we hope will serve as a useful guide for those who are new to the subject area; second, to organise and present the material within a meaningful framework; and, third, to provide a conclusion which draws out the main themes and highlights future questions.

Because our role was one of facilitation and because we wish the voices of the men to be heard without unnecessary distractions, we have omitted our prompts and questions. This was not a clear-cut decision, and we recognise that the omission of questions will contribute to loss as well as gain. However, on balance, we believe that their absence helps the reader to focus on the men's stories and their underlying attitudes and thoughts; moreover, it allows for the attribution of meaning by the individual reader. A number of distinct themes emerged from all of the interviews and, accordingly, we have clustered extracts from each of the interviews under particular headings which aggregate related sub-texts. These are: early life experiences; sexual development; education and employment careers; perpetration of abuse; and the 'core programme' and how it was experienced. The core programme is a prison-based treatment programme designed to challenge the distorted thinking that offenders bring to bear on their abusive behaviour.

Chapter 2 attempts to set the scene for the life story chapters by summarising existing knowledge about the sexual victimisation of children. The specific topics covered include the definition and measurement of child sexual abuse, major theories which seek to explain why such abuse occurs, the consequences of child sexual abuse, the characteristics of victims and offenders, and the treatment of convicted offenders.

In Chapter 3, subjects talk about their experiences within their families, their schools and their peer groups. They focus particularly on how those experiences affected them and influenced their attitudes and behaviour, and in doing so provide insight into the development of their concepts of self. Only two of the men reveal their own experiences as the victims of abuse, although all of them refer, to a lesser or greater extent, to poor relationships with other significant adult male figures in their lives.

Chapter 4 is focused on their own sexuality and how their sexual experiences and relationships impacted on their senses of identity as men. It provides an exploration of how these experiences influenced their sexuality, and how this is intertwined with their views of their relationships with their child victims. The degree to which they define those relationships as abusive ranges from complete acceptance to classical denial.

Chapter 5 provides an outline of the men's experiences in school and subsequently in work. Why they chose the particular kind of work, and whether or not it has any link to their abuse other than that of access, is alluded to by several of the subjects. Some of the men also talk about the culture within which they worked and the extent to which it opened the doors to abuse and subsequently helped them to continue abusing. The extracts highlight direct collusion as well as illustrations of how difficult some colleagues find it to confront what might be an awful and uncomfortable truth.

Chapter 6 provides insight into how victims were chosen and drawn into the abusive relationship. The men reveal, sometimes with intention, sometimes without, the distorted ways in which they justify their actions. Because in the interviews themselves we were not so much concerned with the actual detail of the offending, but rather with the relationships and their contexts, there is little of an explicit nature. However, the pain and damage experienced by their victims is never far from the surface, and manifests itself through the descriptions of the processes of manipulation and despite the reconstructions of the relationships themselves.

In Chapter 7 the men who have been through the core programme present their views on its value and explore its omissions, and what else might be done to screen out potential abusers from some work situations and also to help those currently in such jobs. Their reactions to the programme are mixed, and ambiguity is a feature to be seen in some individual accounts. Perhaps the more significant clues to the impact or otherwise of the programme are to be found in the stories themselves and the manner of their reconstruction.

Finally, in Chapter 8 we attempt to draw out key themes from preceding chapters and discuss their implications for the treatment of offenders and the protection of potential victims of child sexual abuse.

2 CURRENT KNOWLEDGE ON CHILD SEXUAL ABUSE

In this chapter we review the literature on key topics in the field of child sexual abuse. The material presented was compiled primarily for those with limited prior knowledge of the subject area. We start by examining the crucial, and related, issues of what constitutes sexual crime and how child sexual abuse should be defined. We then consider the extent of such abuse, which involves a discussion of the findings of prevalence studies and how these compare with the impression of the problem conveyed by official statistics. In the next section we outline three influential perspectives on why child sexual abuse occurs: feminist, cognitive/behavioural and integrative theories. This is followed by a review of studies on the short- and long-term consequences of child sexual abuse, together with research on the characteristics of victims. We begin the final section by looking at the corresponding research on the characteristics of perpetrators, and move on to examine typologies of offenders, the prevalence of paedophilia, and the treatment of offenders within the British criminal justice system. The latter includes an outline of the principles and aims of the 'core' treatment programme. The views of the men interviewed about this programme are presented in Chapter 7.

Defining Sexual Abuse

The way child sexual abuse is defined is far from being a sterile, 'academic' issue. On the contrary, definitions are crucial. Attempts to assess the true level of child sexual abuse require some agreement on those acts that are to be defined as sexual offences against children. However, despite widespread unanimity that sex between adults and children is undesirable, there is no consensus as to what 'sexual abuse' means (La Fontaine, 1990). There appear to be marked anomalies in how the general public defines sexual abuse

(Finkelhor, 1984). Moreover, definitions of sexual crime have been bitterly fought over by experts from the fields of psychology, biology and sociology, whose divergent academic and political viewpoints have tended to vitiate the kind of balanced discussion that might produce informed consensus.

The problems of delineating child sexual abuse are mirrored in the difficulties associated with the meaning of sexual crime. The law relating to sexual behaviour is often confused, and there is little agreement as to what should be placed in the category of 'sexual' crime. Indeed, English law makes no formal distinction between sexual and non-sexual offending. The Sexual Offences Act 1956, which comes closest to a formal list of offences and provides the basis of Home Office statistics, distinguishes between 12 separate categories of notifiable offence: buggery, indecent assault on a male, indecency between males, rape, indecent assault on a female, unlawful sexual intercourse (USI) with a girl under 13, USI with a girl under 16, incest, procuration, abduction, bigamy, and gross indecency with a child.

A revised version of the list specifies 43 distinct criminal offences involving sex. Because some provisions create more than one offence, the total number of possible sexual offences runs into several hundreds. Moreover, the list can hardly be said to offer a coherent definition of sexual crime. For example, the list includes offences involving sexual acts such as buggery and rape, offences motivated by sex but where no sexual act has occurred (abduction), and offences which are less directly related to sex (bigamy and procuration). Certain behaviours, flagellation for example, constitute offences because of the nature of the act; some, like rape, because they entail a lack of consent. Other behaviours are offences because of the nature of the victim – bestiality, for instance. Age is the key factor in some offences – sexual intercourse is legal between a man of 20 and a girl of 16 if the latter consents, but illegal if the girl is 15. Yet other offences hinge on the location only – consenting homosexual sex involving males over 21 is legal in private but an offence in public places.

In addition to all this, the list includes behaviours such as bigamy which seem to have little to do with sex. Equally, although the position of offences pertaining to prostitution seem more complicated in that they contain important sexual elements, they are also more related to economic necessity than sex. On the other hand, the Home Office list excludes a large number of offences, such as indecent exposure, which may involve a vital sexual component. Further, some have called for a broader definition of what constitutes sexual crime with regard to certain behaviours. It has, for instance, been proposed that all heterosexual sexual activity 'not initiated by women' should be classed as rape. Others have argued that the list includes 'crimes' without victims and that its scope should be reduced rather than increased. For example, there is currently a campaign to have the age of consent for homosexual sex lowered to 16 as is the case with heterosexual sex. It should be added that the legal age of consent varies between countries. There may be significant differences between neighbouring states, as is the case within the European Union. For example, by contrast with the UK, the age of consent for both hetero- and homosexual sex in Italy is 14, while in Spain it is 12.

Some would like to dispense with the notion of a legal age of consent altogether. In support of this view, a magazine entitled *Understanding Paedophilia*, published by the Paedophile Information Exchange, included articles arguing that sex between adults and children is healthy, positive, natural, normal and does not require explanation. It was said that the law should intervene only in cases involving 'the use of threats, violence, unreasonable coercion, drugs, etc.' (Sampson, 1994).

These claims lie at the core of the debate about what constitutes sexual crime. Notwithstanding the anger and revulsion that such arguments engender, it seems that they cannot be effectively countered simply by reference to traditional notions of 'normality' and 'morality'. Paedophilia, homosexuality and incest appear to have been relatively common in both ancient and contemporary societies, including Christian societies of the Western world. Nevertheless, as Sampson (1994, p. 5) argues, there remains a basic distinction between 'sex which is deviant or illegal and sexual abuse, between behaviour which produces victims and behaviour which does not. Unless a sexual act is freely entered into with full and informed consent, or if its consequences are seriously harmful, then it ... should be classified as a sexual crime.' Seen from this perspective, rape and all non-consensual sex constitute sexual abuse, but consensual, non-exploitative homosexual activity does not.

Finkelhor (1984) rightly refutes the paedophile claim that sex between adults and children is freely entered into and fully consensual. He considers that, although sex between adults and children may be less coercive than rape because children may appear to consent passively or even cooperate, children are incapable of truly consenting to sex with adults. For consent to occur, two conditions must prevail. A person must know what it is that he or she is consenting to, and must have true freedom to say yes or no. It is clear that children cannot fulfil these conditions in relation to sex with adults. Children cannot give genuine consent to an activity about which they are often extremely ignorant, or when they have not developed the emotional maturity to deal with the experience. What is presented as free consent on the part of the child is often unwilling consent gained by threats and manipulation.

Further, the paedophile contentions that sex between adults and children is not harmful, and that many children find it a positive and pleasurable experience, do not stand up against the overwhelming evidence to the contrary. Finkelhor (1984) shows that the vast majority of children who have had sexual experiences with adults do not view it as having been a positive experience. Indeed the impact on survivor's lives is often devastating and has been linked with later psychiatric problems, homelessness and prostitution. It also appears that survivors of abuse experience sexual problems later on (Finkelhor, 1984).

The distinction between sexual abuse and non-abusive illegal sex offers a firm basis for the intervention of the legal system in sex between adults and children (or older children and younger children). But the strength of this rationale diminishes as the children concerned become older and gain in knowledge and emotional maturity. It is also weaker in relation to consensual under-age sex between children of the same age which does not involve abuse of power and authority and is not associated with adverse after-effects.

Having distinguished sexual abuse from non-abusive illegal sex, we are now in a position to further examine what is meant by 'child sexual abuse'. La Fontaine (1990, p. 41) employs the phrase to denote: 'adult or sexual activities involving bodily contact with a child or adolescent for ... [the] ... gratification of the adult'. The term 'bodily contacts' includes: 'fondling, genital stimulation, oral and/or anal intercourse as well as vaginal intercourse'. This definition of child sexual abuse entails two key elements: first, it is an adult activity; second, it involves a child as victim. Further, the definition of offender and victim hinges on the ages of those concerned rather than their relationship. In other words, it includes both intra-familial and extra-familial abuse. The definition does not, however, include suggestive behaviour, sexual innuendo or exhibitionism ('flashing'). While clearly unpleasant and potentially emotionally damaging for children, La Fontaine states that many view such behaviours as less serious and quite distinct from the sexual activities previously referred to. La Fontaine also maintains that there is no evidence that such behaviours lead on to the more serious kinds of sexual abuse. By contrast, she reports that even 'mild touching' may signal the start of 'an involvement which is much more damaging'.

However, Glaser and Frosh (1988) offer a broader, more comprehensive, definition of child sexual abuse. They declare:

> Any child below the age of consent may be deemed to have been sexually abused when a sexually mature person has, by design or by neglect of their usual societal or specific responsibilities in relation to the child, engaged or permitted the engagement of that child in any activity of a sexual nature which is intended to lead to the sexual gratification of the sexually mature person. This definition pertains whether or not there is discernible harmful outcome in the short-term.

This definition is useful in that it defines a child by reference to the age of consent, and includes both intra-familial and extra-familial abuse and non-contact activities such as exposure to obscene or pornographic material; it also affirms that the judgement of whether an act is sexually abusive or not should not be determined by its apparent effects. Parenthetically, however, the meaning of 'sexually mature' remains unclear.

The Extent of Child Sexual Abuse

The Cleveland controversy not only raised questions about how suspected cases of child sexual abuse should be dealt with, but also about the extent of this form of abuse. The inquiry report highlighted the lack of reliable estimates for the UK and recommended that attention be given to measuring the scale of the problem (Butler-Sloss, 1988, Recommendation 1, p. 245). The report acknowledged the importance of such data for the work of child protection services.

Attempts to measure child sexual abuse take the form of either *prevalence* or *incidence* studies. Essentially, studies of the prevalence of child sexual abuse estimate the proportion of adults who have experienced such abuse during childhood. By contrast, incidence studies estimate the number of cases of child sexual abuse per year. Typically, estimates of incidence are based on the number of cases known to the relevant professionals: doctors, therapists, social workers and the police. Thus, incidence studies only include cases which have been identified or reported. Because the tabooed nature of child sexual abuse impedes discovery and deters reporting, known cases are very likely to represent only a small proportion of the total number of cases among the general population (Rush, 1980; Finkelhor, 1986; La Fontaine, 1990; Ghate and Spencer, 1995). Alternatives to establishing incidence, such as a nationwide survey of children, are currently thought to entail insurmountable ethical problems. Although retrospective, prevalence studies offer estimates of past and relatively recent levels of abuse among the general population, and allow changes in levels to be assessed over time. Also, because prevalence estimates are based on community samples, they are likely to include cases of abuse which do not come to the notice of child protection agencies. Thus, of the two approaches, prevalence studies are thought to provide a closer estimate of the 'true' rate of child sexual abuse (Ghate and Spencer, 1995).

Most research studies on the prevalence of child sexual abuse have been carried out in the United States. These studies present a rather confusing picture of the extent of the problem. Finkelhor (1986) found that the estimated rates of child sexual abuse produced by prevalence studies in the US varied from 6 to 62 per cent for females and 3 to 31 per cent for males. According to Finkelhor, a number of factors account for this variation.

1. The lack of standard definitions of child sexual abuse. A number of studies are based on broad definitions, others adopt narrow definitions. For example, some definitions include non-contact and extra-familial abuse, others do not.

2. The lack of a standard upper age limit. Some researchers use an upper age limit of 15, others 18.

3. Disagreement about the age difference between the abused child and the perpetrator. Some investigators employ 5- and 10-year age differences, others do not include age difference as a defining factor.

4. Different samples. Some studies involve samples of college students only, while others include subjects of varying ages and from different social backgrounds.

5. Different forms of data collection. Some studies adopt face-to-face interviews undertaken by trained interviewers. This technique appears to elicit a higher rate of reported abuse than more impersonal approaches.

Finkelhor and his associates (1990) carried out a national survey of the US in 1985 during which 1,481 women and 1,145 men were interviewed by telephone. The definition of sexual abuse employed by the researchers included contact and non-contact abuse by another person. Twenty-seven per cent of the women disclosed a history of sexual abuse as compared with 16 per cent of the men interviewed. Some 19 per cent of the female victims and 62 per cent of the male victims had experienced actual or attempted sexual intercourse. An estimated 29 per cent of female victims had been abused by family members against 11 per cent of the boys. Forty per cent of the male victims had been abused by strangers compared with 21 per cent of female victims.

It is plain from the prevalence studies carried out in the US that child sexual abuse is much more widespread than was thought to be the case 15 years ago. If anything, studies are likely to underestimate the true rate of child sexual abuse owing to the stigma attached to it, and because survivors are likely to have repressed their memory of it. Studies carried out in Britain confirm that child abuse is far more prevalent than was previously imagined (Birchall, 1989). For example, Nash and West's (1985) study of 315 young women and students in Cambridge suggests that around half of all women experience some form of sexual abuse as children, although it seems that much of this abuse is of a kind that would not be considered to require intra-familial intervention by child protection agencies.

A more conservative estimate of the prevalence of child sexual abuse in Britain resulted from a MORI poll survey based on a representative sample of 2,019 people of all ages over 15 (Baker and Duncan, 1985). The poll asked people whether they had ever experienced sexual abuse before the age of 16. The following broad definition of sexual abuse was used:

A child (i.e. under sixteen) is sexually abused when another person, who is sexually mature, involves the child in other activities which the other person expects to lead to their arousal. This might involve intercourse, touching, exposure of the sexual organs, showing pornographic material or talking about sexual things in an erotic way.

Of those questioned, 105 said that they had been sexually abused (12 per cent of women and 8 per cent of men); of which 14 per cent had been abused within their own families (1.3 per cent of the sample), 51 per cent (4.8 per cent of the sample) had been abused by strangers and 35 per cent by someone they knew but who was not a relation. A little over half said that the abuse they had experienced did not involve physical contact. Nine people (0.45 per cent of the sample) said that they had been subjected to incest involving sexual intercourse with a relative.

These estimates are undoubtedly much lower than those typically provided by American studies. Having reviewed both the British and American research, La Fontaine (1988) concludes that the best estimate of the overall extra- and intra-familial prevalence rate of child sexual abuse is 10 per cent. Significantly, this refers to contact abuse only. However, La Fontaine (1988) also considers that the available research shows that the sexual abuse of children is not a negligible issue, nor a matter of public hysteria, but rather a serious social problem; further, that even the lowest prevalence estimates serve to indicate that a large number of children experience sexual abuse.

It may also be inferred that most cases of child sexual abuse do not come to the notice of child protection agencies. Although sexual abuse registrations have shown an exponential increase in Britain (Birchall, 1989), the number of children on child protection registers as a consequence of sexual abuse is just 0.05 per 1,000 (Corby, 1993). By contrast, the conservative estimates provided by the MORI poll indicate a prevalence rate for intra-family abuse alone of 13 per 1,000, with an incest rate of 4 per 1,000. Even such prudent figures clearly far exceed the official incidence rates.

Theories of Sexual Abuse

Perhaps the most puzzling question about child sexual abuse is quite simply: why would someone do it? Although there is a growing body of theory which seeks to provide an answer, there are four important caveats that should be borne in mind when considering the research on which such explanations are founded. First, because most child sexual abuse never comes to the notice of the authorities, conclusions based on in-depth studies of convicted sex offenders or survivors of sexual abuse are undermined by the unrepresentative nature of their samples. Second, because perpetrators are generally very reluctant to give accounts of their offending, those who appear prepared to do so constitute an even more unrepresentative sample and what they say must be treated with great caution. Third, because most research into child sexual abuse is carried out in North America much care must be exercised when

assessing whether it may be valid for Britain also. Fourth, because
the methodology adopted by different researchers varies considerably, findings are seldom directly comparable; thus only tentative
conclusions may be drawn when comparing the results of different
studies.

In addition to utilising contrasting methodological approaches,
those who have sought explanations for child sexual abuse have
adopted a broad range of theoretical perspectives which often conflict with, rather than complement, one another. None of the theories that are advanced for such abuse satisfactorily explain the full
range of sexual offences against children. In what follows, three
influential schools of thought on the causes of child sexual abuse
will be examined: feminist, cognitive/behavioural and integrative
theories. The first perspective explains sexual crime by power and
gender relationships in society, the second by the psychological
functioning of individual offenders, and the third combines
elements from the previous two as well as other theories.

The feminist view

The feminist perspective has established itself as one of the most
influential contemporary accounts of why sexual abuse occurs.
Dominelli (1986, p. 12), for instance, states that:

> abuse in the form of violence against women is a normal fea-
> ture of patriarchal relations. It is a major vehicle men use in
> controlling women. As such it is the norm not an aberration.
> The rising incidence of child sexual abuse reveals the extent to
> which men are prepared to wield sexual violence as a major
> weapon in asserting their authority over women.

On this sociological view, sexual abuse is an extreme example of
institutionalised male power over females, rather than a manifesta-
tion of individual (or, indeed, family) pathology. It is argued that men
abuse children because of the general power imbalance between the
genders and the contrasting nature of socialisation that they experience as a consequence. In policy terms, therefore, sexual abuse must
be addressed at a societal level as well as at the individual level
(Rush, 1980; Dominelli, 1986; Macleod and Saraga, 1988).

Feminist theory has made a significant contribution in opening
up a dimension that had previously been missing from explanations about why child sexual abuse occurs. Comprehending and

challenging the nature of male–female power relations, at an institutional level, is of major importance in the theory and practice of child protection work. However, there is a danger that feminist theory can be used in a reductionist and exclusive way, whereby every social ill is attributed to patriarchy (Corby, 1993). More specifically, it may be noted that feminist theory is unable to satisfactorily explain the diversity of human sexual desire and the fact that some men are sexually aroused primarily by children or other men; nor does it adequately account for the (comparatively rare) examples of sexual offending by women (Finkelhor et al., 1988; Elliott, 1993), except where women have been coerced into such behaviour by men. Moreover, equating sexual assaults exclusively with male power fails to take account of those instances where females use positions of power to abuse.

The cognitive/behavioural explanation

The feminist perspective is unable to sufficiently account for the actions of individual offenders and how they might be reformed. For this, one must refer to the various, and often conflicting, psychological theories. Of these, the cognitive/behavioural explanations of sexual offending propagated by Bandura and others have been predominant for some years now (Bandura, 1965). In essence, this perspective views sexually abusive behaviour as behaviour that has been learned. Abusers come to associate certain kinds of stimuli, such as sexual images of children, with sexual gratification, perhaps as a consequence of sexual experiences during their own childhoods. This sexual orientation is reinforced through masturbation to fantasies of child abuse and bolstered by belief systems intended to provide a rationalisation for abusive behaviour. These belief systems violate the sexual ethics and moral standards of society as a whole and include ideas such as: children can consent to and enjoy sex with adults and sex between children and adults is natural, healthy and positive. In part, these views are gained and reinforced through contact with other abusers who hold similar convictions, but they also stem from the outlook of the wider society that, for example, condones the availability of child pornography.

The belief systems referred to are not only used by abusers to justify their behaviour but also to minimise any guilt that they might experience. Sampson (1994) discusses this in relation to the indications from research that many abusers claim to have been abused themselves as children. The 'cycle of abuse' theory holds that victims become abusers, which then creates more victims and more abusers. Incidentally, this not only offers an explanation for sexual offending, but also provides those who campaign to raise public awareness of child sexual abuse with a potent argument to justify engaging in work with both victims and offenders.

However, Sampson (1994) cautions that the tendency of abusers to report childhood abuse and link that to their behaviour may only be a method of explaining their offences and minimising their guilt. He argues that the fact that many sexual offenders report experiences of sexual abuse does not necessarily demonstrate a causal link with their later offending; other factors may be involved. He also points out that the 'cycle of abuse' theory cannot account for the observation that whilst there are a large number of victims of sexual abuse – most of who are female, there appear to be far fewer abusers – most of whom are male. In addition, although some victims may take on the identity and behaviour of a sexual abuser, the process of learning how to become an abuser would appear to require more than exposure to abuse.

Even so, the cognitive/behavioural analysis of how abusive behaviour develops, and is reinforced, is a compelling one. It helps to explain why some adults are sexually attracted to children, and holds out the vital promise that abusive behaviour can be changed – that what has been learned can be unlearned. It has the advantage of being grounded in empirical research; and its analysis of the belief systems which sustain and reinforce offending has a good deal in common with the feminist perspective on the causes of child sexual abuse.

An integrated perspective

Both of the perspectives so far outlined – feminist and cognitive/behavioural – have contributed something to our understanding of the causes of child sexual abuse. Equally, however, both fail to satisfactorily address the complexity of abusive behaviour and the diversity of those who sexually abuse children. It may also be noted that the two perspectives are not mutually exclusive. Recent years have seen the development of approaches which go some way towards combining elements from different schools to provide a more powerful explanatory theory of child sexual abuse. Two of these – Marshall and Barbaree's (1990) integrated theory of sexual abuse and Finkelhor's (1984) multi-factor analysis of abusive behaviour – have been particularly influential and directly underpin most of the work that is carried out with sex offenders in Britain. Both analyses suggest that a range of psychological and socio-structural factors contribute to child sexual abuse.

For Marshall and Barbaree (1990), males have a biological drive towards their own sexual fulfilment and also tend to confuse sex and aggression. Learning how to control these tendencies represents a key developmental task for males. However, poorly socialised individuals, or those who have suffered damaging childhood experiences, can become aggressive and insensitive to the needs and wishes of other people. Feelings of social inadequacy result in hostility towards others. Those who lack self-esteem learn to demonstrate their masculinity through aggressive sex or abuse. Sociological variables also influence abusive behaviour. The norms of sexual behaviour, attitudes towards women and children, the general level of tolerance shown towards sexual abuse and the availability of pornography, all affect an individual's tendency to commit acts of sexual abuse. In addition, some abusers will consciously set about creating opportunities to offend, while others are more reactive and wait for opportunities to arise or respond to certain situations or stimuli – stress or anger, alcohol or drugs.

Finkelhor's model of sexual abuse was specifically formulated to explain the sexual victimisation of children by adults, and stemmed from his perception that there was a need for new theory in this field. He observed that existing theory was not sufficiently able to account for the known facts about child sexual abuse, nor far-reaching enough to guide the development of new empirical research. Two types of theory were prevalent, one was a collection of partially developed ideas about what creates a child abuser, the other was a highly specific family-systems model of father–daughter incest.

Finkelhor (1984) discerned a number of shortcomings with the existing level of theoretical development. First, current theories were not useful for collating what was known about offenders with what was known about victims and their families. This owed much to the fact that research and theory on offenders had been developed by psychologists working with incarcerated abusers in isolation from other workers who were protecting and treating children. Second, currently available theories were not comprehensive. Theories about offenders had been developed mostly from work with men who sexually abused multiple children outside their own families. By contrast, family systems theories had been developed almost exclusively from work with father–daughter incest families. In fact, much sexual victimisation of children, such as abuse committed by older brothers, uncles, and neighbours, falls outside both domains. Third, the prevailing theories tended to neglect sociological factors as most had been developed from clinical work geared to direct therapeutic interventions. However, sexual abuse as a widespread social phenomenon has sociological dimensions that have to be included in theory.

In order to address these shortcomings, Finkelhor (1984) developed a new theory of child sexual abuse which brings together knowledge about offenders, victims and families. He refers to his theory as the 'four-preconditions model' because it delineates a four-stage process through which offenders pass when committing acts of abuse: (i) motivation, (ii) overcoming internal inhibitors, (iii) overcoming external inhibitors, and (iv) overcoming the resistance of the victim.

A potential offender must first be motivated to abuse a child. Finkelhor (1984) suggests that there are three components to the source of this motivation:

(i) emotional congruence – relating sexually to the child satisfies some important sexual need;

(ii) sexual arousal – the child comes to be the potential source of sexual gratification;

(iii) blockage – alternative sources of sexual gratification are not available, or are less satisfying.

The second precondition to sexual abuse requires the potential offender to overcome internal inhibitions against acting on that motivation. Abusers' own internal inhibitions, their moral scruples, can be surmounted by the use of alcohol, or may be undermined where an abuser suffers from psychosis, impulse disorder, senility, stress, or a failure of the incest inhibition mechanism in family dynamics. Internal inhibitors may also be weakened by wider social factors such as apparent toleration of sexual interest in children, weak criminal sanctions against abusers, the ideology of patriarchal prerogatives for fathers, and social toleration of deviance committed while intoxicated.

Third, the potential offender must overcome external impediments to committing sexual abuse. He must gain access to a victim and also have the opportunity to abuse. Both conditions may be easily met in the case of incest or intra-familial abuse. However, in non-familial abuse opportunities must be pursued more actively.

Many child abusers consciously plan opportunities to gain access to children. They seek out venues where children are gathered, and cultivate acquaintance with those who have children. A large number of those convicted of child sexual abuse committed their offences while employed as teachers, youth leaders, and so on. Thus, it may well be that such individuals offend not because they eventually give in to temptation after lengthy periods in the company of children, but rather because they deliberately sought out positions with children so that they could engage in sexual abuse.

Finally, the child's potential resistance to sexual abuse must be overcome. Many abusers are in positions of power or trust in relation to their victims, which makes it easier to overcome such resistance. Abusers may employ threats, coercion, violence, bribery and reward to obtain the compliance of their victims. Resistance will also be easier to overcome where the child is isolated or deprived, ignorant of sexual matters, and lacking the requisite knowledge or confidence to resist. Many abusers report 'grooming' their victims and may be very adept at obtaining compliance and ensuring that the child stays silent later on.

The strengths of Finkelhor's four-preconditions model include the following:

1. It combines psychological and sociological explanations of child sexual abuse.

2. It is at a sufficiently general level to integrate all forms of intra- and extra-familial sexual abuse.

3. It suggests that abuse both by fathers and by paedophiles require an explanation of how the sexual interest in the child arose, why there were no effective inhibitors, and why a child's resistance was either absent or insufficient.

4. It applies both to offenders whose deviant behaviour results from a deviant sexual preference for children ('fixated' offenders) and to those whose behaviour is situationally induced and occurs in the context of a normal sexual preference structure ('regressed' offenders).

5. It puts responsibility for abuse in perspective and, unlike some explanations, does not remove responsibility from the offender and displace it on to victims, third parties or society as a whole.

6. It has direct implications for working with abusive families and individuals in showing that evaluation and intervention can operate at four separate sites to prevent sexual abuse from re-occurring.

Victims

The consequences of sexual abuse

The moving accounts of women who were sexually victimised during childhood have increased awareness and sensitivity about the adverse consequences of sexual abuse (see, for example, Rush, 1980 and Spring, 1987). These narratives have also helped to fuel a growing body of research on the short- and long-term effects of abuse. There are undoubted weaknesses in this research and findings must be interpreted with due care. Despite its limitations, however, research on child sexual abuse represents the best formal knowledge on the problem and, as such, merits consideration here.

In terms of short-term or initial effects on children, sexual abuse has been linked with a range of emotional and behavioural problems, including: general psychopathology, fearfulness, depression, withdrawal and suicide, hostility and aggression, low self-esteem, guilt and shame, physical symptoms, running away and other 'acting out' disorders, cognitive disability, developmental delay and poor school performance, as well as inappropriate sexual behaviour.

However, Corby (1993) draws two conclusions from studies on the initial effects of sexual abuse. First, while a substantial number of sexually abused children experience emotional and behavioural problems in the two years following abuse compared with children who have not been abused, the link between these problems and sexual abuse is somewhat weak and could be accounted for by other factors. The only clear direct outcome appears to be that of inappropriately sexualised behaviour which occurs in between a quarter and a third of all sexually victimised children. Second, sexual abuse *per se* does not appear to have an incapacitating effect in the short term for most children.

Corby (1993) further states that the linkages between sexual abuse and emotional and behavioural difficulties are even more problematic in relation to long-term effects. This is because of the much greater length of time between the abuse and the observed behaviour problems, and because of the possible effect of a much larger number of intervening variables. Nevertheless, research confirms that women who have been sexually abused as children are more likely than other women to encounter difficulties in relation to fear, anxiety, self-esteem, depression, and sexual satisfaction. They are also more vulnerable to further abuse. Thus, it is clear that child sexual abuse can have a serious adverse effect on long-term mental health.

The research evidence indicates that sexual abuse is likely to be most harmful in cases where:

1. The abusive act involved penetration.

2. The abuse has persisted for some time.

3. The abuser is a father figure.

4. The abuse is accompanied by violence, force and/or the threat of it.

5. The response of the child's family is negative.

The age and sex of victims may also have an impact on outcome, but the nature of these relationships is not clear. Nor is there adequate data on the impact of intervention by child protection agencies to show whether this positively or negatively affects the outcome for victims. However, despite its potentially very harmful consequences, Corby (1993) affirms that, contrary to the assumption of many professionals, sexual abuse of children is not necessarily incapacitating to them in later life. This is an encouraging conclusion for those who are concerned with helping victims to become survivors.

Who is abused?

In an attempt to inform preventive policies and practice, a good deal of attention has been devoted to identifying which children are vulnerable to abuse. This has resulted in an accumulation of studies on the sex and age of victims.

It is clear from both prevalence and incidence studies that girls are more likely to be sexually victimised than boys. A study by Russell (1984) appears to suggest that over half of all women are subject to some form of sexual abuse prior to reaching the age of 18. Although by no means all such cases would require intervention from child protection agencies, Russell's study also indicates that around 16 per cent of women experience some form of incestuous abuse, two-thirds of which can be regarded as very serious or serious. Research by Finkelhor and Korbin (1988) indicates that female children are more vulnerable to abuse than male children in the poorer countries of the Southern hemisphere. Official statistics suggest that the same is true in the Northern hemisphere. For example, figures provided by the Department of Health in England show that in the 12 months prior to 31 March 1989 an estimated 0.55 per 1,000 girls, as compared with 0.15 per 1,000 boys, were placed on the child protection registers (Department of Health, 1990).

Estimates produced by incidence and prevalence studies can also be usefully employed in tandem when examining a second key variable in child sexual abuse: the age of victims. The following Department of Health (1990) figures show the age breakdown of children placed on child protection registers in England during the 12 months preceding 31 March 1989:

0.07 per 1,000 under 1 year,
0.24 per 1,000 1–4 years,
0.36 per 1,000 5–9 years,
0.46 per 1,000 10–15 years,
0.20 per 1,000 16 years and over.

These figures show that the peak ages for registration were 10–15 years. Finkelhor (1986) and his associates discovered that the most common age at which both boys and girls begin to experience abuse is between 8 and 12 years of age. This appears to square with the widely held view that many reported cases of child sexual abuse may have a lengthy prior history. It should also be emphasised that much younger children may be subjected to child sexual abuse, as indicated by the official statistics presented above and by prevalence studies (Finkelhor, 1984).

However, as Finkelhor (1984) notes, facts about the sex and age of victims are not sufficient to account for why some children suffer abuse and others do not. This requires information about such questions as whether victims are mainly from certain social class or ethnic backgrounds, whether they tend to live in particular kinds of households and families, and whether they share common life experiences.

Finkelhor (1984) addresses such questions in his research on 796 college students. Some 19 per cent of the women and 9 per cent of the men in the sample had experienced some kind of sexual victimisation during childhood. Sexual victimisation was defined in terms of sexual encounters involving children below 13 years with persons at least 5 years older than themselves and children of 13–16 with persons at least 10 years older. Sexual encounters could involve intercourse, oral–genital contact, fondling or an encounter with an exhibitionist.

Because there were too few boy victims, Finkelhor's analysis is necessarily confined to girls. His findings were used to construct *The Sexual Abuse Risk Factor Checklist*. This proved effective in helping to identify children at risk of sexual victimisation. The checklist includes eight of the strongest independent predictors of sexual victimisation, which are as follows:

1. Having a stepfather.

2. Had ever lived without mother.

3. Not close to mother.

4. Mother never finished high school.

5. Mother with punitive attitude to sexual matters.

6. No physical affection received from father.

7. Household with income under $10,000.

8. Only two friends or fewer in childhood.

It may be noted that having a stepfather more than doubled a girl's vulnerability; almost half the girls with stepfathers were sexually abused. However, the perpetrator was not always the stepfather. Also worth highlighting is the finding that sexual abuse and physical abuse were not found to be related. Moreover, religion, ethnicity, family size, and overcrowding were also not associated with sexual abuse.

Two-thirds of those with five or more of the factors listed above had been victimised. The presence of each additional factor increased a child's vulnerability by between 10 per cent and 20 per cent. The relationship was strikingly linear. Finkelhor warns, however, that the checklist should not be seen as an instrument for predicting precisely in advance who will be sexually victimised, and he is sceptical about the possibility or appropriateness of ever devising such a screening test for either sexual or physical abuse. Still,

such devices can inform professionals about the sorts of backgrounds which put children at risk of victimisation. They can also
serve as tools for further research and theory building about the
causes of abuse.

Offenders

Characteristics of offenders

The issue of which children are most vulnerable to abuse is closely
related to the question of who does the abusing. This matter has
attracted much interest from researchers on the grounds that if
parents and others who are likely to sexually abuse can be identified, appropriate steps can be taken to protect children at risk.

A major concern has been the gender of those who sexually victimise children. As noted above, most acts of child sexual abuse are
committed by men. Finkelhor (1984) estimates that 95 per cent of
girls and 80 per cent of boys are sexually abused by males. Only one
of the 114 women who reported having been sexually abused in Nash
and West's (1985) study had been abused by a woman. Similarly, of
the 411 sexually abused children referred to the Great Ormond Street
Hospital for Sick children between 1980 and 1986, only 2 per cent
had been victimised by women (Ben-Tovim et al., 1988).

Of late, however, more attention has been paid to abuse by
women (Finkelhor et al., 1988; Banning, 1989; Krug, 1989; Elliot,
1993; Adshead et al., 1994; Howitt, 1995; Siradjian, 1996). While,
as in other studies of child sexual abuse, the majority of the perpetrators in Finkelhor's (1988) survey of abuse in day care settings
were men (60 per cent), 40 per cent of the abusers were women.
Yet, as Finkelhor (1988) notes, this finding is not unexpected given
that women comprised the vast majority of day care staff. In his
view, it is more surprising that men, who represent a small proportion of day care workers, commit a disproportionate amount of
abuse. Yet, the high number of female abusers in day care indicates
that an understanding of sexual abuse by women is vital for understanding child sexual abuse in day care settings.

Adshead and her colleagues also state that female abusers are a
group who would merit closer and more detailed study. They argue
that:

such a study would provide information that may have implications for prevention of abuse in the future ... An increase in

recognition and understanding of female sexual offenders might [also] make it easier for victims to disclose their experiences and gain help ... [Moreover], until there is full recognition of the extent of women's capacity to be both aggressive and abusive, the stereotype of the women who are always trustworthy and kind and never unpleasant will continue to exist ... The stereotype is harmful to men and women in general, but especially to victims of abuse by women, who know better. (Adshead et al., 1994, p. 54)

However, although we need to know more about female perpetrators, this should not be used to mask the fact that all the available evidence suggests that the vast majority of child sex abusers are men. Indeed, 99 per cent of the 501 perpetrators recently studied in Scotland were men ranging in age from 10 to 81. Not surprisingly, therefore, the most common age was 40 (Dobash et al., 1993; Waterhouse et al., 1994). Often, however, the perpetrator is a child or adolescent. One study estimated that some 20 per cent of all child sexual abuse incidents in the US involve adolescent offenders (Davis and Leitenberg, 1987). The recent Scottish study reinforces the view that young people are responsible for a significant proportion of child sexual abuse. Of 430 cases where age was noted, some 20 per cent of abusers were aged 15–24 years, with a further 4 per cent aged under 15 (Dobash et al., 1993; Waterhouse et al., 1994).

The age characteristics of abusers offer some insight into the nature of their offending. Howitt (1995) distinguishes three peaks in the distribution of offenders' ages:

1. The adolescent group – largely characterised by an immaturity of psycho-sexual maturation, which results in sexual interest in younger people. The victims of this age group average 6.6 years. Most of these offenders will probably move on to age-appropriate sexual partners, but some will not.

2. The middle-aged group – socially involved with their own and friends' children. The victims of this group average 11 years of age.

3. The old-age group – many have ceased sexual activity and become increasingly socially withdrawn. This group may be inclined to children other than through proximity or organic defects such as senility. Many appear more comfortable with children than with adults.

Research suggests that child sexual abuse occurs at all levels of society. Finkelhor et al. (1986) affirm that class, ethnic composition and regional factors do not appear to affect the incidence of child sexual abuse in the US. In Britain, the MORI poll survey found no significant differences between the abused, non-abused and refused-to-answer groups with regard to social class and areas of residence (Baker and Duncan, 1985). Although the majority of families who come to the notice of the NSPCC as a result of child sexual abuse are relatively poor (Creighton and Noyes, 1989), this probably reflects the fact that state surveillance of child abuse is focused on disadvantaged socio-economic groups.

As previously indicated, much concern has centred on the issue of the possible intergenerational transmission of abuse (see, for example, Briggs, 1995). Studies of male perpetrators seem to indicate that high proportions of these men were themselves sexually victimised as children. In the Scottish study referred to above, of the 213 cases where the relevant information was available, 12 per cent had been the victims of sexual abuse only, and 23 per cent had been the victims of sexual and/or physical abuse as children (Dobash et al., 1993; Waterhouse et al., 1994). Johnson (1988) found that 49 per cent of perpetrators of sexual abuse had themselves been abused. In a second investigation, all the young female sexual offenders that Johnson studied were found to have been sexually abused (Johnson, 1989). Many of the children in the two studies had also been physically abused. However, although there is clearly some intergenerational linking in sexual abuse, the notion of intergenerational transmission is problematic. As we saw earlier, there may be a tendency for abusers to report childhood abuse and link that to their behaviour in order to explain their offences and minimise their guilt. Further, the fact that many sexual offenders report experience of sexual abuse does not necessarily demonstrate a causal link with their later offending. Nor do the majority of victims, who are mostly female, become abusers. Thus, while continuities do exist, the question that needs to be addressed is not whether abused children become abusive parents, but rather under what conditions the transmission of abuse is likely to take place.

One possible factor in this might be the changing shape of the family and the effect this may have on child care practices and children's behaviour. Lone parenthood is increasing; about a third of marriages end in divorce and substantial numbers of children live in reconstituted families (see Halsey, 1988). Two aspects of family structure have received particular attention in relation to child sexual abuse: lone parenthood and step-parenting.

Children in lone-parent families appear to be more at risk from all forms of abuse and neglect than those who live with two parents. Creighton and Noyes (1989) found that a fifth of children registered for sexual abuse were from lone-female headed homes. Although one might expect such children to be safer from abuse by males in such situations, Finkelhor (1986) considers that children in lone-female headed households could be exposed to a greater number of male adult figures than those in two-parent households, and that this could place them at a statistically greater risk of being sexually abused.

It also appears that children are more at risk of being sexually abused if they live with a stepfather. As reported earlier, Finkelhor (1984) found that having a stepfather more than doubled a girl's vulnerability to sexual abuse. Almost half the girls with stepfathers were sexually abused, although the perpetrator was not always the stepfather. Russell (1984) found that of the 930 women in her study, 17 per cent (1 in 6) of those who had lived with a stepfather during childhood had been sexually victimised by him. The comparable figure for biological fathers was 2 per cent (1 in 40).

However, the possible benefits of lone-parenting and step-parenting should not be overlooked. For example, one of the advantages of lone-parenting might be the potential for less interpersonal conflict between spouses. Moreover, step-parents can, and very often do, make an extremely valuable and worthwhile contribution to the well-being and happiness of their children. Further, even on the basis of Russell's high figures of stepfather abuse, 5 out of 6 stepfathers do not sexually abuse their children. Thus, there appears to be a strong case for research on the impact of family structure which takes appropriate account of the positive features and adaptations arising from increasing family diversity.

Contrary to what might be expected, Corby (1993) affirms that researchers have paid little attention to the possible connection between psychological characteristics and child sexual abuse. There appears to be no research linking mental illness with sexual abuse. Although incest has traditionally been associated with low intelligence, there seems to be little evidence to support this (Corby, 1993). As mentioned earlier, however, Finkelhor (1984, p. 37) has raised the following fundamental questions about the personality characteristics of those who sexually victimise children, which require a good deal of further research:

1. Why does a person find relating sexually to a child emotionally gratifying and congruent?

2. Why is a person capable of being sexually aroused by a child?

3. Why is a person blocked in efforts to obtain sexual and emotional gratification from more normatively approved sources?

4. Why is a person not deterred by conventional social inhibitions from having sexual relationships with a child?

More research would perhaps also be helpful with regard to two other factors that have been associated with those who sexually victimise children, namely alcohol and/or drug misuse. As it currently stands, the research data do not support the case for a direct causal connection between alcoholism and child sexual abuse or between drug misuse and sexual abuse (Corby, 1993). However, as previously indicated, abusers may use alcohol or drugs to overcome their own internal inhibitions or their moral scruples (Finkelhor, 1984).

Although there is some research indicating a link between marital or partner problems and child sexual abuse, there are serious doubts about the usefulness of this area of study in the search for predictive factors. For one thing, many adults with children have relationship problems but do not sexually abuse their children. Conversely, sexual abuse may take place with no apparent conflict between the adult carers. There are also problems with regard to defining 'marital or partner problems' and in assessing the quality of relationships. Perhaps a more fruitful line of inquiry would be the connection between violence to women and violence to children (Corby, 1993).

There is evidence which suggests that there is a high rate of reoffending or recidivism among child sexual abusers. However, the studies concerned focus mainly on the worst kind of offender, and we need to know more about the characteristics and circumstances of perpetrators who do not reoffend (Corby, 1993).

Taxonomies of offenders

In an effort to make sense of the complex store of information on offenders, researchers have placed them into broad types sharing common characteristics. The taxonomy which has gained the widest usage in the literature on paedophilia is *fixation* versus *regression*. As indicated, fixated offenders are seen as those whose deviant behaviour is the product of a deviant sexual preference for children. By contrast, it is held that the deviant behaviour of regressed offenders is situationally induced, and that it occurs in the context of a normal sexual preference structure. Some have termed fixated offenders 'paedophiliac', and regressed offenders 'nonpaedophiliac' types. On the one hand, the deviant behaviour of fixated offenders is explained in terms of emotional congruence theory which stresses that such offenders identify with children and appear to want to remain children themselves. On the other hand, the deviant behaviour of regressed offenders is accounted for in terms of blockage theory which stresses that the abusers turn to children sexually as a substitute for their adult relationship which has become conflictual and emotionally unfulfilling (Finkelhor, 1984).

Clear life differences have been found between the two types of offender. For example, a study by Groth and Birbaum (quoted in Howitt, 1995) found that marriage was rare among fixated offenders (only 12 per cent), but common in the regressed type (75 per cent). Strangers or acquaintances were the most frequent victims of fixated offenders (83 per cent of cases), whereas the victims of regressed offenders were more likely to be friends or relatives (53 per cent of cases). The two types of offender committed the same sorts of sexual acts: penetration was equally common and both types operated in a similar manner in terms of rates of seduction and enticement, intimidation and threat, force of attack, etc. However, Howitt (1995) challenges the depiction of regressed offenders as 'normal' heterosexual men who, under the pressures of adult or family life, turn to children for sexual comfort. In his view, this explanation serves to deflect responsibility away from the offender. Howitt (1995) reports that the fixation/regression typology is based on clinical experience with incarcerated offenders which may limit its wider application in the community. Further, the typology has not been validated by research. He also notes that the notion of incest as different from extra-familial abuse is based on three untenable assumptions: (i) that incestuous fathers do not abuse outside the family; (ii) that incest is the sexual expression of non-sexual needs; (iii) that every member of the family makes a psychological contribution to the development and maintenance of sexual abuse. All three assumptions are countered by empirical evidence, and there is a dearth of objective evidence that differentiates incestuous from extra-familial offenders. Howitt (1995) also questions the idea that regressed paedophiles are never homosexuals. Why, he asks, cannot stress or sexual deprivation drive homosexuals to turn to children? He considers that it is the concept of regression which is problematic rather than the nature of heterosexuality.

Knight has proposed a taxonomy of six types of offender where the fixation and social competence aspects of paedophilia are not opposite ends of a continuum as in the fixated versus regressed dichotomy, but totally independent factors (Howitt, 1995). The six types are as follows:

1. Interpersonal – high contact with children (the object-related type who seeks a general relationship with children).

2. Narcissistic – high contact with children but the motivation for contact is exclusively sex; genital activity is usually high in this type.

3. Exploitative – low contact with children; low physical harm.

4. Muted sadistic – again, low contact with children and low physical harm.

5. Non-sadistic aggressive – low contact, high physical damage caused by clumsiness, etc.

6. Sadistic – low contact, high physical damage.

Although typologies have been found to be of limited worth and validity, they nevertheless serve to highlight the problematic nature of some of the conventional ideas about offenders. Typologies are perhaps best seen not as attempts to classify people, but rather the problems they suffer.

Prevalence of paedophilia

As previously shown, it is clear that substantial numbers of children are subject to unwanted and unwarranted sexual experiences with adults. Although there is uncertainty about the precise numbers of abused children – which, as we have seen, depends on factors such as the definition of abuse used, and how and where the research is carried out – useful data are available. By contrast, little is known about the prevalence of paedophilia in the community. Basic information such as the number of active paedophiles in the general population is lacking, and informed discussion of more complex issues such as the number of men with unexpressed paedophile tendencies is currently impossible.

However, notwithstanding its unsatisfactory nature, the limited research that has been undertaken appears to offer rather tentative support for the view that paedophilia is relatively uncommon. For example, separate studies on the distribution of paedophilia-related material available from pornography retailers in the US and Australia found that paedophilia accounted for 1 per cent and 4 per cent of available titles respectively (Howitt, 1995, pp. 30–1). But this does not, by any stretch of the imagination, provide definitive proof of the small scale of active paedophiliac interest in the population. As Howitt (1995, p. 31) argues, 'the question of the extent of paedophiliac interest in the population is a vexed one. It would be of considerable theoretical and practical interest to know how many men keep their paedophiliac urges under control and do not express them through offending.'

Treatment of offenders

While researchers ponder the extent of paedophilia, there is no doubt in the public mind that sexual crime in general, and the sexual abuse of children in particular, are increasing. This belief is apparently confirmed by official statistics which show a significant increase in the officially recorded levels of sexual crime. In England and Wales, for example, reported and recorded cases of unlawful sexual intercourse with girls under 13 rose from 254 in 1980 to 304 by 1990, while reported and recorded cases of incest increased from 312 in 1980 to 435 by 1990. Of course, official statistics are an inaccurate guide to the true prevalence of sexual crime and probably seriously underestimate the real scale of the problem (Sampson, 1994).

Nevertheless, the escalating number of sexual offences reported and recorded in Britain during the 1980s helped to create a 'moral panic' which resulted in a significant hardening of sentencing policy towards sexual offenders. This was characterised by an increasing use of custody. Thus, one-third of those convicted of sexual crime are now sent straight to prison. Of the others, about one-third are fined and a further fifth are either conditionally discharged or receive a suspended prison sentence. Less than 15 per cent receive a community sentence which involves supervision by a probation officer. The proportion of sex offenders placed on probation in 1989 was 12 per cent, which was exactly the same as in 1980. In 1981, there were 1,110 convicted sex offenders in prison; by 1990, the number had risen to 3,000. In 1981 sex offenders made up 4 per cent of the prison population; by 1990, that proportion had increased to 7 per cent (Sampson, 1994).

The increasing use of custody for sex offenders has had a major impact on the prison system. Sex offenders present a unique, twofold challenge to the prison system. In the first place there is the question of how best to protect offenders from attack by other inmates; second, there is the issue of how to ensure that the period spent in prison serves to reduce the possibility of reoffending. With regard to the former, it is commonplace for sex offenders to be on the receiving end of violence and abuse in prison. While antipathy towards 'nonces' or 'beasts' is little more than an idea for many prisoners, some actively persecute those convicted of sexual crimes. The traditional response by the authorities to the threat of abuse and violence has been the use of Prison Rule 43 (or Rule 46, in the case of young offenders). This allows prison governors to order the removal of prisoners from association with other inmates. There is a general assumption among lawyers, police officers and prison staff that all sex offenders automatically go 'on Rule 43' (Sampson, 1994).

The rise in the Rule 43 population has had devastating consequences for the prison system. In part this is because the Prison Service has continued with its traditional interpretation of Rule 43 as meaning total segregation. Such an interpretation requires prisons to run an entirely separate regime for those on Rule 43. However, the general increase in the size of the prison population that has occurred since the late 1970s, along with the gradual reductions in prison officer working hours under the 1987 'Fresh Start' agreement, have circumscribed severely the prison system's ability to provided satisfactory regimes for prisoners on 'normal location', let alone those on Rule 43. Thus, overcrowding and under-resourcing have meant that conditions and regimes for the latter have often been intolerably poor. This is particularly so at local prisons where the use of Rule 43 has been disproportionately high. These institutions have been forced to absorb much of the prison overcrowding of the last 10–15 years, have the poorest physical conditions, and have been particularly affected by the reductions in prison officer working hours (Sampson, 1994).

However, rather than seeking to improve conditions for prisoners on Rule 43 at local prisons, the Prison Service has sought to reduce the numbers of these prisoners seeking the protection of the Rule. This has involved a twofold strategy; first, an attempt to limit prisoners' access to Rule 43, thereby forcing them on to normal location; second, the development of Vulnerable Prisoners'

Units (VPUs). The VPUs quickly became the accepted method of providing protection for sex offenders, and by the end of 1992 there were VPUs at 18 different prisons in England and Wales (Sampson, 1994).

The strategy adopted by the Prison Service for protecting sex offenders has been much criticised for a variety of reasons. In particular, bodies such as the Prison Reform Trust, the National Association of Probation Officers and the Parliamentary All-Party Penal Affairs Group have argued that the reliance on total segregation merely serves to institutionalise and perpetuate the persecution of sex offenders by providing other prisoners with a legitimised target for their frustrations and anger (Sampson, 1994). Sampson argues that although the process of integration would not be an easy one, it would be successful if it were undertaken as part of a more general process of prison reform in line with that proposed by the Woolf Report.

Sampson (1994, p. 99) considers that:

> fairer and more just treatment of prisoners would lower the level of anger and frustration for which persecution of sex offenders is such a tempting outlet. Similarly, purposeful and active regimes would be an outlet for energy and liberal regimes would give potential persecutors something to lose by their misbehaviour. The smaller prison units proposed by Woolf – no unit should be larger than seventy prisoners – would enable closer supervision and the range of specialized regimes these units could offer would enable more flexibility in placement of prisoners.

According to Sampson, such reforms would not only ensure that sex offenders in prison would be adequately protected and able to lead a normal prison life, but they would also address another key issue: 'holding offenders in conditions which increase, rather than reduce, the likelihood that they will commit further offences' (Sampson, 1994, p. 99).

Although the need to protect sex offenders from attack has long been recognised by the Prison Service, the need to tackle the reasons for their offending has only recently been acknowledged in Britain. The lack of coherent attempts at sex offender treatment in British prisons prior to the 1990s contrasted sharply with work undertaken in the Netherlands and Scandinavia, Canada, New Zealand and several states in the US. However, in 1991, following pressure for reform, the then Home Secretary, Kenneth Baker, proposed a new initiative for the treatment of imprisoned offenders.

All sex offenders sentenced to four years or above were to be assessed on sentence to ascertain which were most in need of treatment. The assessment process would take account of offenders' previous history and current offences, their social and sexual functioning, and willingness to participate in the programme. Once offenders had been assessed and had consented to participate in the programme, they would be assigned to one of two types of treatment: the 'core' or the 'extended' programme (Sampson, 1994).

The core programme was to focus on sex offenders' attitudes; it would be run primarily by non-specialist prison staff, often uniformed prison officers or probation officers, with support from prison psychologists. Offenders would usually attend two groups a week over a period of 15 to 20 weeks. The core programme itself was developed by a working party of prison staff towards the end of 1991. It is explicitly grounded in the cognitive behavioural tradition and draws heavily on the work of Finkelhor. As with many treatment programmes in Canada and the US, the core programme focuses on encouraging offenders to take responsibility for their offences and seeks to break down lies and distortions which both justify their actions to themselves and promote later offending. The opening sessions explore the stereotypes offenders have about relationships and norms of sexual behaviour, and move on to examine the effect of offending on victims of sexual crime. This is then related to offenders' own experiences and offences.

The second part of the core programme concentrates on relapse prevention. Offenders are encouraged to explore the circumstances which led up to their offending using an 'offence cycle' model. The group draws up offence cycles for each of its number, identifying particularly high-risk situations (e.g. drinking to excess or socialising with children) which each offender needs to avoid. Each offender formulates a strategy for defusing high-risk situations. All this is documented and a copy is forwarded to the supervising probation officer after the prisoner's release (Sampson, 1994).

In contrast to the core programme, the extended programme entails a high level of specialist input and individual work. It was intended for offenders who represented the greatest risk, the precise nature of treatment being based on the results of the assessment process. For example, some offenders might require work on social skills, alcohol or drug abuse, or temper control, which could be addressed by way of groups led by non-specialist staff. Others might manifest signs of deviant sexual arousal, and would thus require specialist input from psychologists (Sampson, 1994).

However, additional resources were not allocated to cover the cost of implementing the sex offender treatment initiative. The decision at the outset to centre the core programme around groups run by existing, non-specialist, prison staff, was intended to limit the need for more costly specialist input. Yet, the success of the initiative still depended on the recruitment and retention of the requisite specialist staff, and the freeing of non-specialist staff from normal duties. Further, the introduction of the initiative came at a time when the prison system was already overstretched by factors such as persistent overcrowding, cuts in prison officer hours, and by the programme of reforms prompted by the Woolf Report (Sampson, 1994). The lack of adequate resources led to changes in the original line-up of participating institutions and slowed the speed with which individual institutions were able to implement the initiative. By the middle of 1992, it was already clear that the resources available could not guarantee treatment for all convicted sex offenders serving four years.

The timing of treatment under the initiative has also been criticised. It is intended that offenders are offered treatment as soon as possible after sentence rather than at the end. But it is unlikely that the effects of treatment will last from the beginning of a prisoner's sentence until he is finally released. It has also been pointed out that the procedures designed for monitoring and evaluating the effectiveness of the initiative are less than satisfactory, and that the initiative is not sufficiently integrated with the parole and after-care systems (Sampson, 1994).

Thus, despite some indications of progress towards a more considered and planned response to those convicted of child sexual abuse, it would appear that we are currently a long way from a coherent and effective policy. Such was the context of our interviews with the men whose stories are presented in this book.

3 SUBJECTS' EARLY LIFE EXPERIENCES

The theme of this chapter is the early life experiences of subjects as presented by them at interview. The focus is on various life spheres – for instance family, school and peer groups – and how the men's experiences in those spheres shaped their identities.

In discussing their early life experiences, most of the men refer to unhappy or disrupted childhoods, or to childhoods that they perceived as unusual and differing in a negative sense to their own notion of what constitutes a normal, happy childhood. Two of the men recalled having been sexually abused as children by persons outside their families. The childhoods recalled by our subjects vary in terms of factors such as socio-economic class, household composition and culture. Yet, one of the most consistent and striking points that emerges from the extracts which follow is the unsatisfactory relationships which six of the seven men report as having had with their fathers or step or adoptive fathers.

Family Life

KIM

Our first subject recounts early childhood illness, conflict between how he felt people ought to live and his own family's lifestyle, and being unhappy at home which centred on conflict with his sibling. However, it is clear that he specifically refers to his poor relationship with his father as having had a detrimental effect on his development.

I was born in Essex to what was then being classed as a middle-class, fairly well-to-do family. We had a house, and we had a car. I was the youngest son of three. When I was two years old, I had double pneumonia and pleurisy and, as far as the hospital was concerned, would die. But I was ill at home for two years, and was nursed for 24 hours a day, with oxygen and kaolin poultices and I pulled through.

But this caused quite a bit of friction between my eldest brother and myself, in as much that my mother coddled me quite closely and I was getting an awful lot of attention. He was getting not so much attention. Well my brother, he went his own way in life, and I went mine. He thought I was a big cissy and told me so very often. He used to bully me quite a lot. I remember being tied up and tickled on many occasions, which he thought was hilarious, but really it was hell. When he was out with his mates and I came down the street I was in for it. There was a lot of abuse, catcalls and things, you know. Yeah, I was a softie. And even my brother didn't know my sexual leanings – hadn't got a clue. We just weren't that close – end of the road.

I was sort of looked on as the weakling of the family. I was never interested in the macho side of life. I hated sport with a vengeance, didn't like football, cricket, that sort of thing. I went out collecting butterflies, and went fishing. And at that stage I didn't seem to like the middle-classness of my parents and family. They seemed to be keeping up with the Joneses, and mixing with the toffs, as I would put it. And I felt I was mixing at school and things with the less-privileged side of society, and it hit me quite, quite hard. We did all the 'right' things, you know. I always went out in the holiday; we went places, we met people and yet I felt so alone. We had parties, you know, loads of parties at our house, with thirty-odd people, my parents' friends and things. And I felt totally out of it. There was me in the middle of this – loads of people, and I was just – not even a voice, you know. I can remember sitting at table there, and I had a point of view to make, and everybody was totally ignoring me. And I stood on me chair and screamed, you know, 'Someone listen to me', you know. And I was told to shut up and don't be stupid, stop making so much noise. Little things like that, they had a great impact on me.

We're talking war years of course. I was never evacuated, I stayed there. And I think that we were a receiving station for food parcels from Australia, which was supposed to be shared out amongst the poor and needy of Great Britain. And it was always noted by me that all our food stuff was shared out by these friends who could well afford it and who had resources of their own, while their butlers were always starving. These food parcels didn't go to the likes of my mates who needed it. I used to nick it and give it to them. And yet I've never been without food all through my life, and yet I can justify that as not stealing but as sharing out to people it was meant to go to in the first place. Yeah. Just another thing – inequality in life.

I never felt that my father loved me. He never showed any affection to me. He never cuddled me, told me he loved me, anything like that. He was very much a macho man. You know – men shake hands, women kiss. You know, and he knew that I wanted to kiss and cuddle. This was brought home very, very strongly to me when I left home. I was on the station, with all my bags and baggage. Just Mum and Dad were there, and I gave Mum a cuddle and a kiss. I went to cuddle my Dad and he pushed me away – shook my hand, pushed me on the train. I cried all the way down to —— station; that hurt – that's hurt ever since. Little things like that. Job to remember them all; I've pushed most of them away.

I don't think any one of these factors has had a – to my conscious mind – has had a direct impact on me. It's only sitting back while I've been in prison, looking back and thinking 'Well, all these little things added together give me quite a strange bias on life, I suppose'. And yet – you know – up until looking at life. People have said, you know, 'What sort of family life have you had?' and I've said, 'Well not idyllic, but not bad.' And I think, when I had a family, I said to myself, 'these kids are going to get something that I never had'. And my kids have had attention. They've been places with us, we take a total interest in them, give them love and affection. We've let them know it, too.

I always thought that the friends that my parents had were false – that they weren't real friends, that they were friends of convenience; that basically my mother was the key to all this. She was the carer; she cared for me, she cared for everybody. She and I are very similar in a lot of ways. She is the soft, loving, caring person; hard at it. She wasn't soft in that way, but she was soft in nature. And she was the one that volunteered to put on a party for any occasion. She was the one that volunteered to do all the catering, she did all the clearing up afterwards. It was Mum that was the heart of all this – holding all this together. My father was the guy with all the noise, that had a few drinks and was the 'Haw-haw-haw' you know, 'aren't we doing well?' sort of thing, but it was Mum who was actually clearing around in the background, keeping it all together. So he basically financed the thing and kept everybody happy at the parties and it was Mum who was doing the groundwork.

But looking at it, I sort of thought, 'Well, why are all the parties at our house? Why not their houses?' you know. And even if there was an occasional party at their house, it seemed that Mum did all the catering and took all the plates down there! And it didn't seem right. And then the occasion arose later on in life when Dad became ill. I was living up in the country with a young family, and they were living down in Essex. So I was tearing the arse out going backwards and forwards, trying to support Mum. And then we wanted places for Dad to go to recuperate away from home and things and to give Mum a break, because she'd done a 24 hour nursing job in looking after him.

And we found that their group of friends were not too bloody available, like. They all had excuses why they couldn't help. This went on; Dad recovered eventually and then he had a recurring thing – he had a heart attack and he was very low then. And again we wanted the same assistance; no help forthcoming. And later on, Mum died and left Dad on his own and there were no friends at all. ... So my original thoughts were confirmed – that they hadn't got any friends at all. They were just friends of convenience, that were sucking up to what was available. And this has had a huge impact on the way that I have run my life and the friends that I have been with and the friends that have surrounded my home, basically.

I think the main thing in this was the lack of relationship between my father and myself. I did make a desperate effort when I was a kid to try and come up to my father's expectations and what his young son should be, and I joined the school rugby team. Now surprise, surprise, I quite enjoyed playing rugby – a big shock to myself, let alone anybody else. And we played a few games; we got thrashed on many an occasion. My father was never interested in coming to watch a rugby match, whereas he'd go and watch my brother play football, which niggled a bit and I nagged him and nagged him. And one Saturday he actually came to school – it was just a rainy Saturday afternoon. I don't know what the score was, but I scored a try. Now I felt like a dog with two dicks; I played rugby and scored a try in front of my Dad. Now I felt ten foot tall and I came off the pitch and my father's only remark was, 'Bloody cold night, don't understand that silly game you're playing.' You know, even to an imbecile it was quite obvious that I'd done something pretty spectacular out there and there was no sort of recognition of it. And that bloody hurt and that was the end of my rugby.

So, little things like that and that was before the ... when I left home session, you know, which just compounded the whole thing.

So I've sort of nursed this feeling about my father for many years. The only time that my father really sort of felt proud of his son, I felt, was when I achieved success in my career. He then started to sort of warm towards me – it was quite noticeable, amazing. And I felt right sick about that, because I'd achieved an awful lot in my life, in my eyes. You know he didn't think much about me coming through college. I'd been a complete non-achiever at school, but left school and three years afterwards to have got virtually what was now being classed as a degree, I would have thought would have made him happy, but no. So I might have been a disappointment to my father, but I think my father might have been a bit of a disappointment to me as well.

HARRY

Our next subject had been adopted shortly after birth and saw this as having affected his development. He describes his adoptive parents as 'quite elderly' with 'old fashioned' ideas about child-rearing and his adoptive father as 'very, very strict'. He also mentions that his adoptive parents were somewhat distant, partly because of their age and partly because much of their time was devoted to business interests. As transcripts presented later will show, Harry spent a large part of his childhood at boarding school.

I think most people's childhoods have an effect on them and particularly so if they're somewhat unusual and mine was somewhat unusual, in that I was adopted as a baby, so the people that brought me up were – as far as I was concerned – my mother and father, although I later found out they weren't; they were adoptive parents. Also in later life I discovered that I had brothers and sisters which I knew nothing about. So as life went on I discovered all these things which you know ... most children grow up in the family home, and they have one mother, one father, hopefully and you know, it's all very straightforward, and my background seemed anything but.

So that, I think, had an effect on me; I don't know what effect, I wouldn't like to say that to any extent it was responsible for the way I behaved, or I wouldn't want, sort of, to put any blame on the fact that I had a disturbed childhood, or anything like that, but I would certainly go so far as to say that it had an effect on the way that I grew up. I went to boarding school, so I grew up away from a family environment, and I suppose throughout most of my early life I was a bit afraid of people, ... found it very difficult to get on with people.

I was brought up as an only child, because the people that adopted me were quite elderly. They had a daughter who had moved away; she was living in America and only kept contact by letter, so she just didn't exist as far as I was concerned ... I met her once, when I was about eleven or twelve, that's all. So effectively, I was an only child. But I discovered later, as I said, that my natural mother had four other children all a little bit older than me. So that was quite strange, to sort of discover that in later life.

I can't remember much of my very early childhood. I just got a general impression of a very strict father. I mean he wasn't unfair, but very, very strict. They were rather old-fashioned parents; my mother was much more lenient towards me, although if I did do anything wrong it would be up to my father to put that right. You know, chastise me. It wasn't an upbringing without love, but at the same time looking back on it, it was – you know – they were a little bit distant, partly because of their age, and also partly because they were very, very busy in work.

When they adopted me, they were running a pub, my father – well, adoptive father, was working for a business and also running the pub and that was at the end of the war. And so, he was working very hard – he was a workaholic; expected everybody else to work as hard as he did, and through my early childhood he had a succession of jobs and his time was very much taken up with them. My mother had some time for me, although she also worked in the pub, so I didn't see a great deal of her either. I can't remember much of my early childhood; I can remember one or two occasions that obviously had a particular effect on me, like when I was about seven, I think, my father took me on holiday. It was almost unheard of – I know my mother nagged at him for ages and he eventually took me on holiday to Scarborough.

We weren't actually living in Scarborough at the time – we did live there later on – but at this time we were living in, I can't remember exactly where, but it was some little distance from Scarborough. So we went there to stay for just a few days; I think it was about four days, at a boarding house and he would take me to the beach. He would sit on the beach and read and I would play in the sea and so on. And I remember wanting very much a *Beano* annual from a shop. And as we were walking back from the beach – I'd had an ice cream on the beach and I wanted this Beano annual and I remember him saying to me, 'No, you've had your ice cream, that's enough for today.'

VERNON

The transcript which follows recalls a childhood which was heavily disrupted by the Second World War. This involved repeated changes of school and placements with different families. Our subject, Vernon, also reports witnessing death and carnage during the bombing raids. There were, however, also positive aspects to his experience of evacuation. In Vernon's view, it helped to make him independent and also removed him from a very restrictive family, with parents who found it difficult to show emotion and affection. His mother was domineering and 'kept [him] on a tight leash'. His father, by contrast, was 'a quiet, subdued man', who he never really got to know.

My childhood was very disrupted because the war intervened and as a result I had ten changes of school in ten years, which must be something of a world record, and I lived all over the country. I mean, you were simply sort of rounded up at a railway station; you had no idea where you were going, you left your parents behind and you were taken off to some other place in the country. You were taken to some sort of community hall, or store, or something and then local people came along and picked you out and said, 'I'll have that one' and then you went off and lived with them – that was the system. So it was just pure luck, you push or you can't.

When the war broke out, we were living within a mile or so of one of the key military targets. So all the kids in the area were shipped out immediately to the stupidest place they could have sent us because we were right in the middle of the bombers' flight-path. When the German bombers came over to bomb they came straight over us and after bombing they came back again, so I was actually in considerably more danger there than I would have been had I stayed at home. And there was one very big raid on Liverpool – I think it was the biggest daylight raid they ever had. We watched the planes go over and the sky was absolutely black from one horizon to the other with hundreds of aircraft. But of course they moved very slowly in those days, the old Heinkels, and made a terrible row and then of course I'd wake. We small kids, you know, were very interested in all this.

I'd just got home from school one day and these planes were coming back! And there was a little backyard in this house and I was watching; I was standing outside the back door watching and I saw this Heinkel coming over, on fire. And I saw two little black dots come out of it, open up and it was the crew bailing out, you see. And I was absolutely fascinated. So I climbed up on to an old kitchen table that was in the backyard and this plane was coming closer and closer and I suddenly realised that it was going to crash on the house where I was standing! And I was so terrified I couldn't move – I was literally scared stiff. And the woman in the house, was at the sort of kitchen sink, she looked up and she could see what was happening and she grabbed me and took ... there was an underground cellar in this house. We went down to the cellar and we could hear this plane coming and she protected – it was all over in a minute, but it seemed like ages and the noise of it – it had one engine still going – and the noise, you thought even though you screamed at the top of your voice, you wouldn't be heard. And the old lady from next door was there and she was having hysterics which was very upsetting for us all. And then suddenly there was dead silence. We waited, I don't know, half-an-hour, forty minutes, maybe and the all-clear went and we came upstairs thinking that we would find nothing but a pile of bricks and the house was absolutely complete – nothing wrong with it at all. I looked out the back door and there was a bit of broken chimney pot and that was the only damage at all. And so I wrote home and told my mother about this and she was absolutely horrified and decided I had better get back to living with them.

So I went back home and I arrived just in time for the worst bombing raids. And my parents took me, as a special treat, to the cinema – it was only the second time in my life that I had been to a cinema. I can still remember the film. And we went to the early evening performance and as we went into the cinema the air raid sounded and we had paid to go in, all the other people had as well, they wouldn't go out just because there was a raid. They started the film. Things got very noisy, so they stopped the film and a thing came up on the screen advising everybody to go to the air raid shelters immediately. I remember, I was terrified of this film because it showed some kids running through a forest – it was very quiet, you know and it all seemed real to me. And suddenly, a stick of bombs came through the roof, incendiary bombs and fortunately we were seated underneath the balcony, but the people in front of us got it – even up above, and I remember ... I'd rather not talk about it ...

Anyway, as a result of that, I was sent away down to Dorchester, and billeted with a very old lady who was very prim and proper and she didn't like children. And there was me and another boy evacuee with her, and she had a servant who was supposed to look after us. We were desperately unhappy, so I wrote to my mother and she came down and got me transferred to another family in a village just a few miles up the road, where I was much happier.

And then some months later, my father's office was bombed out and they were all evacuated. So it was decided I could go home again. And I went to one school there, then I was transferred to another school, then I was transferred to a third school and then the doodlebug offensive started with the V1s. And we got a lot of them in our area and again we had several very near misses. And it was decided I would have to be evacuated again.

So I was sent off and went up to the Peak District and on to this farm and I stayed there 'til 1947, 1946, well, at least a year after the war, anyway. And I was very happy up there, though I knew nothing about farming at all. I thought it was a foreign culture up there because I just could not understand a word anybody said and in those days the dialects were much stronger than they are now and of course I gradually picked up local lingo and became a farmer's boy. I remember when I was put on a train to go back home, I was worried because I didn't think I would recognise my mother and she was waiting on the station for me and I rushed up to her and said something, and she said 'What the heck are you talking about?' So that was the reason why my education was very badly disrupted by the war. I must have been nine, or nearly nine when I first went away, until about thirteen, fourteen.

I wasn't actually with my parents for some of the more important years because of the war, but my parents were strict Catholics and my mother, who was very much the dominating influence in the family, was not an educated woman. She kept me strongly under her. She was a very big lady, very strict; I was kept on a very tight leash and, I don't know, maybe that was one of the reasons why, at the end of the war, I was living on a farm, a remote farm as an evacuee and I didn't want to go home. So I stayed there until eventually, about a year or so after the war, the government announced that they were not prepared to pay any longer for evacuees and they were all sent home. My parents were – I won't say they were strangers, but I wasn't very close to them, by then. My father was a very quiet, subdued man – I never did get to know him – he didn't really talk about himself.

It probably did me good in a lot of ways, because it got me out of a very tight family. Even as a kid, I wasn't allowed to go out on my own, I wasn't allowed to mix with the common children around. And by the time I came back, I was old enough to have a bit of freedom and so on. And although I respected my parents I don't think that I particularly loved them, because they both of them felt it was degrading I suppose, to show any sort of emotion, to cry or to show affection.

It was a very ordinary sort of suburban family, nothing special about it at all; mother was particularly well off. One extraordinary thing was that I never had any pocket money whatsoever, and if any relatives gave me money for Christmas, I was made to put it in a savings account, I wasn't allowed to spend it. So I never had any money at all, really, until I went to university and got a grant and that seemed like fantastic wealth at the time. I just couldn't believe that I had all that money and as a result of that I have always been very careful with money. I think that's the reason for it. I mean they gave us presents at Christmas time and if we wanted anything badly you could talk them into giving it to you, unless it was something they terribly disapproved of. We did things together as a family, we used to go on holiday together.

Evacuation got me out into the world and I was forced to become more independent. I mean, up on the farm in particular, they had no children. I was left very much on my own, allowed to do what I wanted. I was encouraged to sort of mix with the main homestead to do the necessary jobs, and I was given quite a lot of responsibility. I mean, I had an hour's journey every morning to school on the bus. When I came home in the summer, I used to have to get off at the village which was about a mile away and then round up three dozen short-horn cattle and drive them up the main road to be milked. Then they were kept at the farm until the morning, and because I had to leave early to go to school the farmhand used to drive them back. I certainly didn't worry about it, because there was no traffic. There were no cars during the war. But they didn't see anything remarkable at all in an 11-year-old boy being left with a herd of cows, driving them up and down with the hay. I used to go up in the fields with the horses; I used to be sent round with the sheep – they had a big flock of herding sheep. You had to go round with sheep dip and get the ticks off them using a matchstick which you dipped in the undiluted stuff and so on. I burned all the skin off the side of my face one day doing that.

On another occasion, the one thing I was frightened of was that – they had two horses, and the biggest horse was called Valiant and he was an enormous horse and if I stretched up I could just touch its chin. And on one occasion, we were harnessed in a turnip field one November. We couldn't use tractors because it was too wet, and the horse wouldn't stand still. We had to get these turnips back to chop 'em up to feed to the cattle. And there were flies buzzing round his head, and I was told to hold the horse still. So I reached up and just managed to get hold of the strap under his chin and I was holding on for dear life and just at that moment, the horse tossed its head to get the flies off. I was lifted clean off my feet and Valiant looked at me in surprise, at this small boy sort of hanging on to him, put his foot forward to steady himself and the foot came 'Wallop', right on my foot. And I tried to get my foot out but I couldn't, with the weight of the horse on top of it – terribly painful. One of the things I knew was that farmers' boys never made a fuss; we weren't allowed to make a fuss, so I didn't ask for help or anything. I just pushed and shoved this great hoof and eventually it moved and the whole of my toe and the bones were crushed. And of course, in those days there weren't any phones, National Health Service or anything and we were always needing a doctor anyway, so I just had to grin and bear it. And that's why I can't wear ordinary shoes – had a crushed foot ever since you know.

So, I was left to sort of think for myself. It built me up, and I think it made me quite sort of independent. So I didn't rely on my parents when it came to choosing a career and determining what to do, I sort of made up my own mind.

DAFYDD

Our next subject, Dafydd, remembers the trauma of his mother's divorce. Her re-marriage meant moving home and for our subject, an unhappy relationship with his stepfather. It may also be noted that Dafydd mentioned that he was sexually abused during childhood by a female friend of his parents (this is not contained in the extract which follows).

I had what I thought was a normal, happy childhood. We were a very close family; large family with lots of cousins and aunties and uncles. I'm the middle child; separated from my Dad when young, which was really traumatic – cut up about that, I really idolised him. There was a divorce, Mum had a divorce and then my step-father took the whole family to Australia. That was a real wrench.

I didn't get on very well in school, though I got very, very good reports from my Welsh schools. I loved school in Wales. It was a culture shock, really. No relatives whatsoever, it really was a wrench. My younger brother, he was too young to understand all this – he's grown up Australian.

We moved to a larger town when I was ten. Mum and Dad had got a job running an estate and we had a massive house. So I had my own large bedroom. And Mum and Dad had separate rooms and there were guest rooms and staff rooms – it was just – Wow!

I didn't like my step-dad, I've got to say that. Nothing that I did agreed with him. I went overboard, maybe this is part of my problem; I went overboard in trying to please him. And everything just fell. Nothing at all got his approval. And indeed, quite often, 'You're goddamned useless!' Yes, I picked up on that. Certainly a failure in High School; my biggest achievement in High School, sports-wise, was making the third football team. I mean this was such an important team that sometimes young players didn't even turn up, you know. I couldn't make the first or the second team, just the third team. And this didn't endear Dad to me, nor me to Dad either.

RONNIE

The subject of the following account, Ronnie, vividly recounts the intense pain associated with the rejection and emotional abuse that he suffered from his father (who returned from the war a changed man); how, for example, in middle childhood he desperately wanted his father to hold him, to manifest physical affection towards him; how his father took no interest in his education despite his excellent performance in examinations, which was all the more outstanding given his working-class background.

I was born during the war and I'm told that my father was present at my birth, but within a few weeks he'd gone away. And the next time I really got to know him, I was six years of age. And unfortunately, from the very beginning we never hit it off. I don't know the reasons to be honest, because even in adult life I was never able to get to grips with this situation. But whether it was me rejecting him when he came back – strange person entering our lives, or because I had no brothers or sisters, or what my mother very often said that the man who came back was not the man who went away, I don't know.

But as a result of that I had, partly, a very unhappy childhood. I say partly, because living next-door-but-one to me was my grandmother. And from a very early age I went to her, literally, for breakfast in the morning and stayed with her until bedtime and only went home at bedtime – part of the reason was, we were

living in a very small house. In those years, for some reason, my
father turned on me. I was never abused, either sexually or physically, but once a week, it was Saturday night; I still remember it
with dread, always. I knew he'd be coming home – it was the only
night of the week he went out – and when he came home he had
been drinking. And he would be giving my mother a very hard
time and very often anything to do with me was resented. And
being in a small house I was actually able to hear all these conver-
sations and I used to be terrified; I used to be very frightened at
age nine or ten.

This kind of behaviour pattern, by the way, continued right up
until the age when I was 27, which is quite interesting really –
when I was independent and living away. But as a child, little
things I remember; my best friend at the time had lost his father
during the war and looking back over the years, I still remember a
day we were out playing together and I said to this boy, I actually
said to him, 'I wish I'd been in the same position as you.' And
looking back now, I'm amazed as a child of ten, eleven, that I
should have said such a thing. But I remember that incident as if
it was yesterday.

So in that sense, I had a difficult time. I passed the 11+. He
wasn't willing for me to go to grammar school, but my mother
stated that she would go out to work herself and keep me – which
she did. I came to 15, he wasn't willing for me to continue school.
Again, at my mother's insistence, I continued with my A levels
and went on to college. So you see, even up to that stage of my
life he was still someone who I resented very much indeed.

Finally, in 1968, I had a phone call that he'd suddenly died.
Obviously I came home to organise the funeral and everything. I
still remember my feelings, you know; at a funeral you literally go
up and stand over the grave and I was ashamed of my own feelings. I remember saying – 'Well this bastard won't hurt us any
more.' And I was very ashamed of my own feelings then. Because I
do remember as a young child, a young person maybe ten, eleven,
twelve, that's the time when I say, remember. What I wanted more
than anything was for him to like me. What I wanted more than
anything was for him to touch me, to get hold of me. I've never
had any memory of him ever touching me in my life and I used to
actually remember that very much indeed. Very strange thing in
adult life – and this is even true today – I get very moved if I see a
father with his children, showing affection, all these years later.

So that's the background to that relationship. My mother made
up for it for me; she was a hard, hard-working woman. And as I

say, as a child, right up to the time I was an adult, I used to spend virtually all day with my grandparents. They became a kind of second set of parents to me – guided me through secondary school. So that I wasn't deprived in the sense I didn't have a male role-model to look to – my grandfather was that male role-model. He was, he took almost the part of what a father should be, in my eyes. That was my kind of background.

Because I had such a hard time with my own father, I should then have ended up being a better father than anybody else in the world. In a sense that I never, ever – this is the crazy part of it you see – he never sexually abused me, he never physically abused me. He abused me tremendously mentally, yet I've done the opposite. I've never mentally abused anybody, I've never hurt anybody. I've gone out of my way to be nice – to give comfort and listen to people. I've been a very good listener and that's it. I've done all those things he didn't do. And yet I've also done those things he didn't do. Sexual – I haven't used any physical abuse, I've never hurt anybody in that way. I don't know, I'm still mixed up about that. I can still feel how I was as an eight-, nine-, ten-, eleven-, twelve-year-old, I wanted him to hold me – not sexually I mean, though I didn't know what sexual meant; I wanted him to physically hold me. I remember that. Of course that was always rejected. I don't think I even shook hands with him ever. This is the crazy part of it.

When he left the forces he had quite a good job. He became ill and he was advised that he had to have job in the open air, so he became a farm labourer. And eventually he was the farm manager. So he was a hard-working man; a man, by the way, in his own field, very respected by his employers – very hard-working person. Outside the house he was a respected person. His brothers and sisters – well his brothers all died before they were 60 – all had cancer; his sister still lives. None of them ever knew, have ever known today how he treated my mother and myself. There's a phrase: devil round the hearth, but an angel in the street. He was highly respected. And nobody outside knew what we were going through. Nobody else knew, not even the next-door neighbours knew. Because my mother looked upon it as a shame to accept that this cruelty was going on. And I never told any of my friends, not even as a teenager, not even as a young adult. In fact I didn't even tell the girlfriend I was going with for such a long period of time. I couldn't bring myself to tell anybody; I was ashamed of it. It's very strange looking back, why would you be ashamed of some-one being unkind to you? It was just my father you see, I wanted something, I wanted something that was there, perhaps from him

and in the end, all fathers were things up there, you know –
strange, very strange. But you can't turn the clock back can you, in
any relationship, be it if you're angry or want to turn it round?
That's what hurts as well, that you can't put things right.

JAMES

*There is, of course, a danger of reading too much into the sorts of
account presented above in terms of the possible relationship between early childhood experience and later acts of child sexual
abuse. The extract which follows may help temper any tendency to
do this in that the subject, James, remembers his childhood as an
essentially happy one. James begins with a recollection of being a
rebellious child. He also recalls being hospitalised, and that he did
not like school. His parents were strict, but not overly so, and they
were loving. However, James was one of two subjects who reported
having been a victim of sexual abuse as a child. Moreover, he sees
a direct link between being sexually abused himself as a child and
the acts of sexual abuse which he later committed.*

At school I was this very rebellious child. Every society has a very
rebellious child; a little bit anti-authority, wouldn't want to know
why if somebody said, 'Don't do that James!' My very first reaction
would be, you know, that was school, absolutely hated it. I didn't
want to be there. Absolutely didn't see the point. Wanted to be at
home – very much a Mummy's boy, judging from what I've been
told by my parents. I had appendicitis when I was very small and I
was taken in to have the operation, but on this particular day I
had a cold, you see. And obviously they couldn't perform the operation if I had a cold, so I was kept in hospital – I don't remember this at all. Obviously in those days your parents weren't allowed to stay with you. Mum said, 'it was the first time you'd ever
been away from us. By the time you were in bed you screamed and
you wouldn't stop, no matter what anybody did, even when I came
in you would still just scream.'
    Generally, I think I had a very happy childhood; very support-
ive, fairly strict, but not overly so. We had a fair amount of freedom. Mum and Dad set standards and having set them we were
expected to appreciate them. I can always remember my Mum. I
always think of my home as a kid, as one that's full of laughter;
that's the vital childhood memory. There were always people there
and it was always warm and full of laughter, with me sort of trying

to push and see exactly how far I could go. If I was given an easy shot then I'd try and take another inch, you know.

My parents are very close as a couple. They obviously both went through the war as older teenagers or young adults. I think that coloured their view of the world profoundly. Discipline was quite important within the home, but in a sort of loving, caring way – not just strict authoritarian, you know – you will do this because I am the adult and I say you're going to do it. You know, they always did try and explain, 'Well done, you know, you can't stick your hand in the fire, because you'll burn yourself and it hurts and it damages you!' I can remember obviously they had their quarrels and arguments and what have you, but these always seemed to be patched up very quickly, and it was always in front of us as well. So it wasn't the sort of you know, 'Shhh, the kids are here', type of thing where you start thinking, 'well what's going on?' It was very much a big explosion and then it would all be over and everything would be back to normal.

DAVID

Our seventh subject recollects being the youngest member of a large working-class family in a Nottinghamshire mining village; how he felt pressurised to conform with norms of macho working-class male culture; and how this conflicted with his desire for intellectual and spiritual development. He also reports physical abuse at the hands of his older siblings.

I should imagine that the biggest influence on my early life would have been my culture, my background within the family situation; having grown up as an only child, but within an extended family living within my grandmother's home; I suppose that was the main influence in my early days; being the youngest child in a large household. The elder ones were considerably older than me. Yes, becoming the youngest child of brothers, of my mother basically, those were the biggest things to influence my early years. And sharing a large house with a big family. Not really having the rights which a normal household would have. Not having your own home. Always having the matriarchal society of a grandmother being in charge of the system. And also not having the rights of being the only child, which was perhaps a sad wish to want then. Always being the last in the pecking order.

I think that a lot of the pressure which I discovered and identified within myself during my formative years would have resulted from having to conform with the older boys; the older brothers who were my uncles really; and the pressures which came from there. I think there is always a mixture of the culture element there. In a mining village, you had to conform, you had to have the macho sort of image – you had to be one of the lads, one of the gang. And I found it very difficult to blend the fact that I could compete on the physical side with my intellectual side, which wasn't acceptable within that culture.

When I was coming to puberty – 12, 13, 14 – I wanted to express myself. I wanted to be an individual, I didn't want to do what everybody else did. I suppose it just manifested itself in my teenage rebelliousness. Wasn't so much aimed at everyone, but more specifically at my situation where I was living, within the home, or just the larger family. I wanted my own space. I remember not having my own space, not having my own room, having to share a room with one of the younger uncles. And just that sort of feeling, sort of pent-up frustration and anger and all that, which I can identify now. But then it was expressed very much in quarrelling with my uncles; just getting into bother with them, really, and getting punched about and things like that by them, when they had had enough of me, and that sort of thing.

This was not just lads fighting – they could be quite hard punches. But then – that was part of it all you see – you had to take the punches, you'd have to keep it to yourself. It was almost that culture of, 'I can cope with it', but really inside I couldn't cope with it and I knew I couldn't cope with it, which made me more and more rebellious, which meant more and more getting into trouble with them. Finally I sort of dug in and thought, 'Well, they'll be gone soon, getting married, leaving this house', and I determined within myself that I was going to do my own thing at that time, regardless of what anybody else wanted – my own rave-up. I used the ability which I felt I had or knew I had, but which the family didn't know I had, or didn't want me to have. I used what they didn't want me to use as a rebellion against them. And went on from there.

I remember constant tension which has remained with me and, indeed, I suppose in many senses will always remain with me, because it's so ingrained within those years and ingrained within me. I feel you can't unlearn what has been learned in those years, you just have to learn how to cope with it and channel it, I suppose.

School Days

Some of our subjects had more to say about their school days than others. Two recalled hardly anything. The recollections of a third are contained in a transcript presented earlier. It may be noted that our subjects attended a range of schools from local primary and comprehensive schools to grammar and boarding schools. This partly reflects variations in the socio-economic status of their parents. As would be expected, most of our subjects did pretty well at school en route to professional occupations.

KIM

Kim, however, harboured bitter memories of his school days and only achieved educationally after leaving school. He remembers coming 'bottom of the class every year, in every subject except art'.

Oh, I performed with a degree of excellence at school, I came bottom of the class every year, in every subject except art. And that was the only subject that I got any sort of marks for at all. I was not interested in school. Nobody was interested in me. So, I thought, why should I do all this? I wanted to go flying. Nobody bothered to sit down and tell me that I would need maths and English and science and geography. It wasn't until I actually got out there that someone said, 'You'll have to go to college.' And I went there and the whole world suddenly arrived on my doorstep. It was hard going, but the point is that I got through, you know, I got myself through. And so I must have absorbed something way back there, but just didn't want to reproduce it for exam times.

So I was a late starter, basically, educationally. Yeah, I hated school. The happiest day of school was the day I left. My maths was taught by a ruler's edge straight across the back of my knuckles when I got it wrong. It wasn't until I was a good half-way through junior school that they realised that I couldn't see the bloody blackboard in any case; I needed glasses. They didn't even bother to find out – there you go. And at the time they just put it down as a normal part of everybody's life. And I suppose it is – but where's the funny ending?

HARRY

Harry recalls a succession of different boarding schools, all seemingly unsatisfactory in one way or another, before moving to the local comprehensive school at the age of 12 following the death of his father. His recollections of significant events at boarding school include the memory of an inappropriate physical chastisement by a schoolmaster.

The reason I went to boarding school was because I wanted to. I'd read 'Gems' at school and had some romantic notion that it was going to be wonderful; of course it wasn't, but I had a marvellous notion that it was going to be, you know, much better to go away to a boarding school and in some ways it was, but also it was very hard. The first one that I went to was dreadful. When my mother came to visit me after I'd been there for a little while, she saw how run-down the place was and the fact that they were using the children to actually do the cleaning and the polishing and all that sort of thing rather than employ domestic servants; she got me out of there very quickly.

I went to another one, which was a bit better and then finally to quite a good one. The academic side was at least adequate, I would say. And it was much, much better run – although this was, you know, just after the war, so things generally weren't that brilliant. But it wasn't at all badly run and although it was a bit spartan at times, I think we were very, very lucky in actual fact, so I quite enjoyed that. But then my father died and we went to live in —— where I finished my schooling.

I actually quite enjoyed my first school, although it was gruesome really; it was very tumbledown – it was a danger. Peter Sellers did a skit about a public school. Some parents are looking at a photograph of the school and they say that the fire escape doesn't look very safe. Peter Sellers comes back with, 'It's a lot safer on the photograph than it is on the building!' And, I mean, it was exactly like that. They had a swimming pool, which in their brochure they made a big thing about. Well, you wouldn't have dared to have gone in, because it was filthy. It was a pond and it was dangerous, there was that much mud in it – I mean it was incredibly run-down. My parents had sent me there without, you know, actually examining it and like I say when my mother finally fetched up there to visit me, she was actually horrified at the state of the place. But I actually quite enjoyed it.

The only thing was, I wasn't actually learning anything, because you know the slightest misdemeanour, you were taken out of the classroom – given a job polishing the bannisters or something of that sort. That's how they got their work done and it was incredible that I actually did enjoy it there. I mean apart from it being, you know, fairly strict in the class, we had quite a lot of fun. We had a lot of the grounds to ourselves. There wasn't much discipline outside of the classroom, so you had your dormitory. Matron used to come round and check up on you and things like that, but you could have midnight feasts and nobody came round after about nine o'clock at night. And during the daytime and at weekends you could go for walks; you could go where you wanted virtually, with very little limit on what we could do.

It wasn't at all structured; there were games of football, but it was very sort of ad hoc. If you wanted a game of football, you just went down to the pitch and found a few others who wanted a game of football, you know, nothing was organised about the place at all. And I mean, the work was easy, because in class you tended to be doing very simple things anyway. I can't remember ever being the slightest bit challenged there. I wasn't there all that long, so I can't really remember. But unlike the other schools I went to, I didn't find any of the work the least bit challenging at all – very, very easy – it was sort of like repetition, and that was about it.

I remember being very glad to be home from my first boarding school and sort of telling them some of the things that I didn't like about boarding school. But then I think most children are like that, you know, that the grass is always greener on the other side and when you're at boarding school you want to be home; and when you're at home, you want to get back to boarding school. So it was about like that, you know, there wasn't any sort of great problem with me being at boarding school. On the whole it was a nice place.

I can remember a bonfire night at the boarding school. I can remember a huge bonfire, and remember being impressed by the fact that for three days afterwards, the ashes were still hot. Don't know why that should stick in my mind particularly, but it does. I can remember there being acres and acres of grounds which we weren't allowed to walk in, which distressed me enormously, because I always loved the countryside and liked walking. There was a lake there, which we weren't allowed to go near. Once a year we used to beat the bounds and then the whole school could go all the way round and that was great, but for the rest of the year you weren't allowed to go in those places, which I thought was a bit of a waste. I remember one occasion, it was my birthday and our housemaster, a Mr Greenham, was a bit kinky actually and he certainly liked smacking people. And I was playing on a pile of sand – there was some builders' sand there – and I was playing on it and he saw me and took great exception to the fact that I was actually running a little toy car over the sand. And he dragged me inside and was going to give me a good thrashing and I remember this other lad interposing himself between us and saying, you know, 'It's his birthday, leave him alone.' There are one or two incidents I remember, like sticking chewing gum in somebody's hair, you know, things like that. That pretty much covers what I can really remember of my early childhood.

VERNON

It may be recalled that Vernon's education was severely disrupted by evacuation during the war, which meant repeated changes of school. From the following transcript it seems that he overcame this problem by his own ability and determination to succeed, combined with the benefits associated with an educative home environment. His father and siblings were academically able, and the house contained a large collection of books.

Fortunately, the war finished just before the crucial time, so I had a couple of years to prepare for my exams. It wasn't GCSEs in those days – School Certificates they called them. And those years were reasonably settled. And all the family were, I wouldn't say intellectuals, but they did fine, apart from my mother. My father had a university degree. He was very interested in literature, that sort of thing, and he had an enormous library. My brother and sisters were similarly minded. I didn't do as well as my brother but I managed to get into university. I realised that, you know, unless I did so, I was never going to earn much money. I barely had any money of my own, and I got quite interested in school work in the last two years or so and I think I worked pretty hard actually. In fact that's the reason I wear glasses. In the sixth form I had to start wearing glasses.

DAVID

David vividly recalls his struggle to reconcile the conflict between his working-class home environment and his desire for educational attainment. For example, he recalls having completed and signed the forms regarding choice of O levels himself, and telling his parents that his examination results were significantly lower than they actually were. His determination to escape from disadvantage meant reconciling the conflicting demands and expectations of home and school. This necessitated cunning, secrecy, deceit even, but also inner strength; it also meant being able to endure, indeed embrace, isolation. Our subject carried over this capacity into his professional life in the church. Here too it was an advantage, and it remains a boon in prison.

I found it very hard at the beginning to, if I can put it this way, to play as a D-stream boy, but academically to be performing as an A-stream boy; and having that dichotomy of roles. That period exerted a large influence on my life. It was very much the thing then to break from the mould and go on to achieve academically. I had a very difficult task trying to convince my parents, and perhaps the family, that I wanted to pursue academic things rather than get a job, do well and earn lots of money, which was the obvious thing to do. So that was perhaps the main influence in my background, together with my decision to be part of the Church in a family with no sort of religious background.

I remember having to get things for myself, having to make my own choices. I did stupid things like filling in the O level selection form as I wanted and not taking the forms home, and signing my parents' signatures on the bottom and choosing the subjects I wanted to do, regardless of what they felt was necessary for a good career as a tradesman, where I could make lots of money. Instead, I opted for more academically based subjects, rather than practical based subjects. It sounds stupid, actually going home and not giving my exam results or giving exam results which were lower than I had; it was just a silly game really, but it was a game which at least, for once, I had control of. It was part of my life which I could control because it was outside family.

This is what I wanted to do, this is where I wanted to go and by fair means or foul, I was going to get there, basically. I just saw it very much as a game. There were important decisions which I was making as a 13-, 14-, 15-year-old which perhaps, most 13-, 14-, 15-year-olds would discuss with their parents. I was in isolation. That would be a word which I could identify with very easily through my upbringing and through my work, basically. I was very much on my own within my chosen profession. It's a profession where you work on your own, really. I am a loner, I suppose; a loner who liked society, found company, found community, but I am very happy with my own company, having built the resources within myself as a youngster to survive and to maintain who I was in a culture which tried to make me something else. And so, even now, I find my ability to be alone is a great resource to have here, as you've a lot, quite a lot of time of your own; I find it quite a strength. I'm never bored on my own, but I'm often bored in company.

School was a completely different culture from home, a different culture altogether; it was sort of a city culture rather than a village culture. It was a big school – there must have been more people in the school than there were in the village. There was a wonderful sense of anonymity, whereas at home everybody knew everybody, back to the fourth or fifth generation. School culture was a faster culture – it was a more exciting culture, it was a much more creative culture; I found it exciting and challenging and demanding and one which I thrived on really. And the more I went to the school, the more I discovered how much what I thought of as family culture, and great, and all that, was deficient in so many ways. And again, that contributed to feelings of isolation at home, feelings of rebelliousness against the system; feelings, also I think of having lost out because of the family, blaming them when I wasn't having the same situations at home that I was in school.

School was a large comprehensive for boys, a crazy old sort of place, you know, where you – because it was a large boys' school – had to be alert and alive to yourself and everything else; lots of competition, lots of good competition, I mean; lots of very good friendships; lots of very good opportunities to do what you wanted to do really; teachers related well to you, if you related well to them. I still know some of the staff now; some of them are, well, my contemporaries.

The conflict between home and school life experienced by David is to some degree mirrored by the experiences recalled by Ronnie in an earlier transcript. Ronnie too had a difficult time. He passed the 11+, but his father was unwilling to allow him to go on to grammar school. In Ronnie's case, however, his mother intervened on his behalf, and went out to work specifically in order to earn sufficient money to support her son at grammar school. Later on, his mother further insisted, against the wishes of his father, that he be allowed to stay on at school and complete A levels prior to going on to college.

Peer Relationships

The transcripts presented below appear to reveal a seemingly rather unusual pattern of peer relationships among the men interviewed. Kim mentions having been introduced to homosexual activities by a primary school peer. Harry, who spent much of his childhood at boarding school, recalls the inappropriate punishments with sexual overtones that were inflicted by a particular housemaster. He also remembers having been the object of much bullying, and seems to have been generally rather isolated from the majority of his peers. Vernon also appears to have been somewhat isolated from his peers, which he links to the effects of the war-time evacuation. David too experienced problems in his relationship with peers. In his case, he felt obliged to conform with macho, working-class, norms. This required him to subdue or suppress his own personality, which he regards as having had a significant long-term impact on his development and behaviour.

KIM

Kim appears to refer to having been introduced to sex by a friend that he met on his first day at infant school. He reminisces about the mischief that the pair got up to, their shared sense of being rebels, outsiders, alienated from their own families. Kim also refers to his parents' rejection and hostility towards the friends he chose for himself, which he attributes to snobbishness on their part.

My earliest proper memory I suppose, was my first day at infant school; we were all filing into class, all in pairs; holding hands with a stranger by the side of you, getting to know you. My oppo was a guy called Billy, and we became firm friends from that moment onwards. And I suppose, I don't know where he learned it from, but I suppose I learned my sex from him. Basically, I was introduced to it and we stayed firm buddies and we were kicking around doing everything that wasn't legal. We did all sorts of things; we went swimming in the canal in the nude; and, oh dear, pinched apples off greengrocers. If there was trouble around, it was Billy and I, we were into it. And we were, you know, we were bosom buddies, right the way through until I left home, basically, and then we drifted apart. But everything I did was with Billy.

Yeah, even ran away from home with Billy – broke into my money box and took all my savings and we got as far as —— before our money ran out and we went home hungry. There you go.

Got into more trouble over that – was banned from seeing Billy – but he was my first real friend. And he and I seemed to think alike; he wasn't much accepted at home either, because he wasn't part of our society, so to speak. So that was my first sort of kick, that my parents didn't accept other people and that rather hurt. Now, their friends had to be my friends, so why couldn't my friends be their friends? I couldn't adjust to that. When challenged about it, you know, it was, 'Oh I don't want those dirty little things crawling round my house', sort of thing. 'Don't know where they've been' and I couldn't understand this. They were good enough for me, I could see nothing wrong with them, but not my parents.

So, I suppose I had my full realisation of class distinction and it hurt and that stayed with me all my life. I have been definitely anti-class, you know; I hated class distinction, colour, race, creed – it doesn't bother me.

HARRY

Harry, who spent much of his childhood at boarding school, recol-lects that he was bullied at school. He was considered 'a bit of a softie', was seen as a bookworm, adopted a superior attitude to-wards his peers, and tended to associate only with boys who he saw as being among the more intelligent of his peers. He mentions that these relationships were 'not necessarily sexually orientated'. He refers to a special friendship with a boy called Jim, which later transcripts reveal to have had a sexual dimension. He also refers to a housemaster who appeared to enjoy inflicting inappropriate physi-cal punishments on the boys. Harry refers to the housemaster as 'kinky', but makes it plain that he and the majority of his peers accepted such practices as part and parcel of school life.

There was a bit of bullying, I remember that; I can remember sort of being picked on a bit, probably because I was top of the class, you know, nobody likes a bookworm – it wasn't too bad. I was in the scouts – liked that; I liked sort of outdoor activities and liked the adventure of it, you know, making fires in the open, all that sort of thing. And liked the camaraderie of it. I was a bit superior; I think I was probably quite obnoxious at that age. I suppose I had a bit of a superiority complex in some ways and I tended to have fairly close relationships, not necessarily sexually orientated, but close affinities with other boys who were reasonably well educated, you know, reasonably intelligent, because I found it easier to sort of get on with those. I found some of them rather uncouth. I sound like an awful snob, don't I? But I suppose I was at that time, and I found it a little bit difficult to get on with some of the others. And in fact because, thinking about it, because of the way the classes were structured, you had your 4A, 4B, 4C, and so on. Because I was in 4A, it was only children who were reasonably intelligent anyway that I would have day-to-day contact with. Everybody looked down on 4D, and 4E – I mean, they were practically animals, sort of thing. Thinking about it, it's a rather bad system, because you then get this sort of strata, don't you? You know, where the children in the upper classes sort of, are looking down on the others and can't see that they've in fact got abilities that they haven't. But anyway that's by the by.

At the time, I certainly felt, as I think most of us did, that we just didn't want anything to do with those that were in B, never mind about C, D and E. So you tended to have your own little cliques and I tended to enjoy the company of those who had a sense of adventure. And we'd go down by the river a lot and try to build boats – although I was never much interested in fishing. The only sort of fishing I used to do was with Jim. We used to walk along by the river and if we saw somebody fishing where they shouldn't be, we'd pretend to be farmers' sons and confiscate their catch, and things like that. But as for sitting on a cold river bank, you know, for hour after hour – didn't really seem much fun.

The bullying at school wasn't too serious. I didn't like physical activity, you know, like boxing or anything like that. We had to do boxing and because I was fairly tall, I was always partnered with the other lad in the class who was also tall, who was the school boxing champion. So I used to get rather knocked about when we had boxing and I didn't like that at all. Didn't particularly like rugger; we only played it a few times, but I didn't like that. I liked football and I liked cricket and I didn't mind running and things like that, but anything that involved actual physical violence, I didn't like. And I suppose I was considered a bit of a softie – maybe partly deserved, as well. I certainly didn't mind rucking in, but I couldn't see the point of sort of hitting someone, you know, and letting them hit you – even worse; it just seemed absurd. So I was picked on from time to time, but like I said, nothing terribly serious, more a case of you know, three or four of them sort of jumping on you on your way back from school, or getting your clothes dirty and getting told off when you get home, that sort of thing.

I don't think it had any great effect on me. It wasn't as though I was sort of picked on continually, or as if I went in fear of going to school or anything like that. I think I accepted it as the norm, as just one of those things that you have to put up with, from time to time. And I got on quite well with my peers, you know, with those that were in my own class, the A class. There was no sort of bullying from any of those, it tended to be the bigger lads, the louts from the other classes, who probably picked on quite a few others, you know, that they thought were different to them. But they probably felt because they were physically stronger, that made them superior to us; in the same way that we felt because we were more intelligent than they were, we were superior to them. So, you know, it was probably along those sort of lines, really. None of it was very personal.

The sort of fights that you used to have at boarding school was that another boy would twist your arm behind your back and you'd have to say, 'Uncle'. And if you said, 'Uncle', he'd won; and if you didn't say 'Uncle', it was a question of whether he had the will to break your arm or not. And I tended to win my fights because I just wouldn't say, 'Uncle'. And so they would twist my arm and twist my arm and they'd get to the point where they thought, 'Oh, I'm going to break it if I twist any more' and so they would just throw me away and say, 'Let that be a lesson to you.' And all my friends would clap and roar, 'Well done, well done', you know, that was the way that it was done.

If I thought I was in the right – I'm trying to remember an actual incident, there were very few fights I got into, I mean it didn't happen very often, but it might be something that I perhaps had said to somebody and I felt in the right and they felt aggrieved – I just wouldn't say, 'Uncle' because I knew I was right, sort of thing. But I can't remember an actual incident. But it was very, very rare, I mean that only happened perhaps three or four times in the whole time that I was at boarding school. I believe there was very little sort of violence at all; the only violence I saw was the housemaster, who used to sort of take a delight in smacking and he would tend to get the other children to get involved in it. So instead of just him giving a smack, he'd encourage all the others in the dormitory to grab hold of you and pull your pants down and then you'd get the slipper on the backside, or something like that – it was a bit kinky.

It happened to me a couple of times – don't think it bothered us too much. I do remember there was one lad there that it bothered a lot; I think perhaps he used to get the slipper a bit more often than the others and he complained to his parents about it and, as a result, this housemaster – he's still there, he's still employed by the school – was demoted to a general dogsbody, a caretaker, or something like that. He definitely got a demotion, but he wasn't dismissed, so it wasn't that serious. I suppose you could read things into it and it may have been that he went a lot further with some of the boys than he did with me, I don't know, I'd be speculating. For all we were aware of, it was something and nothing. We thought, 'Well, that's the way things were done, you know, and if he gets his kicks that way, then you know, it's just our hard luck, we had to put up with it', sort of thing.

VERNON

Vernon seems to have been rather isolated from peers as a child. He attributes this to the effects of the evacuation. There was conflict between the evacuees and children from the host communities, his friends from Liverpool were scattered over large areas, and he attended the grammar school while all the other children went to the local school. Nevertheless, Vernon might have been expected to talk about friendships he made at the grammar school. That he did not, tends to confirm the impression that his isolation from peers owed at least something to personal choice, thus reflecting factors within his own personality.

Because we were evacuees, there was a certain cloud of fear in between us and the local kids; they didn't like us much. I can't remember ever getting to know any of the local kids very well, you tended to go around with your own Liverpool friends. But the trouble there was that we got scattered all over the place, to different adoptive parents and most of them went back home after a few weeks anyway. And then of course, when I was up on the farm, I was really very much on my own, because there were no other kids around there at all. And I was the only one that went to the grammar school, all the rest went to a local school, so I never really made any friends when I was there at all. I used to go round with the men.

DAVID

David recalls the intense pressures that he felt to conform with his male working-class peers whose macho, 'survival of the fittest' attitudes conflicted with his own sense of self. This required him to subdue or suppress his own personality and inner values which, in his words, left him 'with a huge problem'. He developed a desire to conform with group norms which he sees as being linked to his later acts of child sexual abuse. This is explained in later transcripts which show that others among his professional colleagues, including more senior colleagues, were engaging in such abuse and these activities appear to have been tacitly accepted as part of the underside of the informal professional culture. He sees his conviction and imprisonment as marking an important watershed in that it has provided him with an opportunity to be true to himself. He also refers to being somewhat isolated from peers in his home environment because he was part of a large family and owing to the fact that his school was located some distance from his home locality. He appears to have been happier among his peers at school.

There were pressures to conform, to do what everybody else was doing, to really subdue one's own ambitions to other people's ambitions. 'Don't do that, do this', I think there was a great pressure to conform to the image of home, of a male in a working-class family, in Nottinghamshire. To look to the club, to sport, to work as my goals in life, and finding that I did not want to do that. But yet finding there was also the peer pressure to do it.

Subduing my own self to other people left me with a huge problem of always wanting to make other people happy and subduing my own needs and wants and desires, in order to be accepted into the group. I find it a very hard thing, even now, to resist the temptation to conform to the group and to keep my mouth shut, to allow things to happen, to just run with the crowd, really. Whereas, my real self is much more individualistic, much more a person who wants to stand up and stand out for what I feel is right and against what is wrong. But I see it as very much a contributory factor, that's something that I've got to cope with now, got to beware about myself.

It would be difficult to explain in terms other than general sort of, 'go and do this, or we will give you a hammering' sort of stories. It's always your turn to be the one to get up to mischief basically, and, if you didn't, then mischief got to you, you know.

They're just general stories really, of loathing, that's all I can say. It's more of a way of life, you just got into it and it just became part of you, became part of your being, because it was easier to do it that way; it was easier to know what they wanted and to perform according to their rules, which is a lot easier for everyone. But I was using my intellect to survive; I knew how they were playing the rules, therefore I'd play by their rules and survive. And it was very much the same when I moved into the large comprehensive school; it was a matter of the fittest survives and you just had to adjust to your environment. I suppose you just get to know the hard boys and you make them your friends. You learn that – I've learnt that from the beginning – make sure that the bullies are on your side, basically.

It was very much this difficulty, or this flaw within myself, of wanting to conform. It is easier to run with them than it is to stand away. Now I find in the situation I'm in – and since my offending brought my conviction – that it is much easier to be myself. I found imprisonment to be a good psychological and sociological break-point, where I've actually had time to sit and look at myself and decide, 'Well no, I will not, I don't want to go that way', because that could have been – and I'm not using it as an excuse – but that could have been a contributory factor to my offending; the fact that it was easier to go along with it, than to stand by what I knew was right and what I knew was wrong. And I also see it as a contributory factor, not an excuse.

Macho culture would have meant for me that you never showed your emotions. Yes, I think emotions would have been the main thing which were suppressed. And on the whole, it would have been more doing macho things all the time, which you didn't particularly want to do; playing sport, getting up to boy-type mischief; you know, fighting, gangs, that sort of thing; just living the image of the street-wise and hard, you know, that sort of thing. I was a part of that upbringing, and that spilled over into my school. I mean, you had to be very street-wise and very hard. So that was very much part of my teenage years. I don't recall much below that, of my earlier years.

My peer group didn't really develop very well. A number of my relationships were with older people, rather than with my peer group. I had contact in school – very good friendships in school. But unfortunately we were bussed 11 miles from home, so you never had the tie-up between home and school; they involved different groups. I was in with a group of friends at school, but at home would revert back to the old rhythm where I'd grown up without relationships and what-have-you. So that again added to the tension between home and school. And if you transfer your thinking, your behaviour, accordingly, the effects of that would be very much that you were very happy in school, but very lonely at home; because at home, as your group, family group, got older, different interests started, girlfriends and what-have-you, and so your group would reduce, by which time it was too late to relate to your peer group, who had already set their relationship patterns. And yet at school you'd be very happy and relate very well with your own group and become a very much more social animal than you would at home. You learn never to tell a sociologist that anything is normal or abnormal, but you'd almost see one as an abnormal situation; and I think I had identified the down at that age as being something I didn't like at home, and the school situation as being something which was good and normal and 'I wish it was like this all the time' – to use a phrase that describes it well. But being the only kid from my particular village who went on the coach to a school some miles away, you never had the opportunity to have those friends as part of your world.

4 SEXUAL DEVELOPMENT

Retaining a focus on early life, the theme of this chapter is our subjects' own sexual development. Through their words, we will explore how their key sexual relationships during their formative years influenced their perceptions of themselves as men.

Two subjects, Dafydd and James, reported having been sexually victimised as children. One felt that this was directly linked to his own sexual offences against children; the other subject did not refer to a direct link between his own victimisation and the sexual offences which he later committed. Nevertheless, it is clear that the impact of the trauma he experienced during childhood remains with him today.

Four of our subjects described themselves as homosexual. Their sexual offences involved boys. However, the offences of two of the other men who did not refer to themselves as homosexual also involved boys.

As will be clear from the transcripts, all the men who discussed their sexual development appear to have encountered difficulties with regard to establishing their sexual identities and associated relationships.

KIM

In discussing his sexual development, Kim states that he was aware of having homosexual inclinations from childhood. This homosexual identity was reinforced through relationships with peers. However, because of negative general attitudes towards homosexuality, outside these relationships he passed himself off as heterosexual. It is clear from other transcripts that Kim lived a double life from middle childhood through to his imprisonment in middle age. Despite being married with two children he continued to engage in homosexual relationships.

I seemed to go out of my way to mix with the less fortunate, rather than mixing with what my parents would call my peers and that's how it's been all my life. I've always sort of sided with the underdog not with the upper class, so to speak. I mixed with a group of lads, I suppose, and I found out at a very early age that I was interested in the males and not the females. I also realised at a very young age that it was not socially acceptable and I developed this smoke-screen.

I was able to pull girls like mad; they went overboard for me and I pandered to their wishes, which looked publicly acceptable, but I was really having my fun with the boys and that has been basically the pattern of my life, right the way through to this, to when I came inside. That was how it went.

At school I had quite an introduction to male homosexuality, but it was with my peers. We had a sex club; we used to go around to one of these guys' houses every week and as soon as we got in the front door, we peeled off our clothes and anything went! There were four of us guys, and one of these guys' younger sisters who was taboo. We weren't allowed to touch her, but she was amongst the crowd. So, anything went and to them, in hindsight, it was just an investigation into, you know, what was around. To me it was something far deeper than that and I got great comfort and joy out of it and so it progressed. And up until when I was sort of twenty-odd, I'd always had a male partner of my peer group.

HARRY

When discussing his sexual development, Harry begins by referring to his relationship with a seemingly rather strict and somewhat distant father, who was preoccupied with work. Although careful not to draw a direct link between the latter and the development of his homosexual identity, Harry does feel that the two may be related in some way. He believes that the roots of his homosexuality were present prior to going to boarding school, and talks about his sexual development and relationships during his school days and as a young adult, all of which he appears to have found unsatisfactory.

My father's word was law. I didn't dare say anything. I remember an incident with the next-door neighbour's girl, who was a couple of years older than me. She took me into the garden shed and wanted to show me hers, to see mine, and we were caught in the act and I remember an enormous fuss. I wasn't actually punished; I think I was sent to bed or something. I wasn't actually smacked or anything like that, but it was considered, you know, a terrible, terrible thing to do. That made a big impression on me; the fact that there was such a reaction to it and I wasn't allowed to talk to her and, you know, there was great animosity between my parents and next-door – it was like that. I can't really remember how we were discovered; I think it was my mother that discovered us, but then told my father about it, but I wouldn't be sure about that. All I can remember is his sort of very – he didn't lose his temper, he didn't sort of go mad or anything like that, but it was just his ... He was the sort of man that if he was displeased with you he only had to look at you in a certain way and it would turn you into, sort of, quivering jelly. He didn't have to raise his voice, but it was just a general feeling of, you know, total disapproval of what had happened.

And it sort of went on as well, it wasn't just then. It was a continuing thing, 'Oh, you mustn't have anything to do with her', and all this sort of thing. I just got the recollection that it went on for some time and that it caused some problems, you know, with them – obviously they were still living next door, so it did cause some ... We did move away after a while, I think. I don't think that was the cause of it, I don't think it was anything as major as that, but my father tended to move around. So we tended not to stay in one place for all that long anyway; tended to move around a lot.

I mean, I loved him but he was sort of a bit distant. Because I didn't see very much of him, it was a sort of love that one has for a figure of authority, rather than for someone that you have very, very close contact with. I don't want to make him sound too distant or, you know, uncaring, he wasn't; it was just that he had so much work most of the time when I was a child old enough to be noticed at all. And he was very ambitious. He wanted to get on in work. He wanted to achieve a great deal. He had a lot of drive and ambition. So although I would see him for some of the time, perhaps of an evening or the weekend, even then, there would still be discussions about work, you know. With my mother also working, it tended to be all rather that. So there was very little time for relaxation.

It's very easy to sort of, you know, pluck things out of the past and say because of that I became a homosexual, you know; didn't sort of get on with women, or whatever; it's a bit easy to sort of say that. I wouldn't go along that road, but I would say that it probably had something to do with it.

I know that when I went to boarding school, the first one I went to when I was only about eight, seven or eight; although I wouldn't have known how to sort of discuss it, or recognise the term homosexual, of course I wouldn't, but I had the feelings there, you know. There was an older boy who took an interest in me and sort of came and tucked me in last thing at night, you know, and he even kissed me goodnight the first few nights. So you know, there was, looking back on it, I'm very sure that the emotional feelings were there right from a very early age. And whether they were cause or effect, you know, I don't think you can really say. I suspect that I was destined to be like that anyway and possibly the circumstances of my childhood may have exacerbated it, I don't know. But I think it was probably there anyway.

Well, at the first school, there weren't really any close relationships. It was at the other school that I went to where there was one boy and that relationship lasted throughout my time at that school, although he was older than me and I think found me a bit of an embarrassment after a while. I tended to sort of hang around with him and follow behind him, like a lost sheep.

There were one or two others there that I got very close to. When I'd been there about a year-and-a-half, the school actually moved from a very old building – although it was in good condition. They moved to a very modern place. They moved quite a considerable distance. There was a big mansion house, but all the rest of it, the bathrooms and everything, was very, very modern – all been purpose built. They'd been planning to move there for some time, but I didn't know that when I joined the school. Anyway, when we moved there we had these very modern dormitories. There were about six of us in each dormitory, and I remember there was a lot of close affection between boys in the same dormitory; nothing sexual, I mean that just didn't enter our heads, but there was a lot of closeness when we went to bed. You'd sort of hold hands with the person in the next bed or something like that. Rather strange, you know, these days, because children of that age today would, you know, be very, very aware, but of course, we weren't. And the sexual side of it, as I say, just never entered our heads. I was sort of 11 at that stage, yes 11, 11 going on 12.

Later on, I went to an ordinary secondary modern where I was in the top class, and top of the class in just about every subject, and tended to take life very easy, just sort of go along at a very relaxed rate. And after I'd been there a very short while, another boy joined the class who had been at the grammar school, but he'd

fallen behind because of some illness, I think. And, because he'd
fallen behind they'd taken him out of the grammar school and put
him in the secondary modern. He was in a very similar position to
myself and the two of us used to sit at the back of the class and
play games and things, you know, and the odd 10 per cent of the
time do the schoolwork, sort of attitude. We had a very superior
attitude to everybody. We thought we could do it standing on our
heads; most of the time we could, but some of the time we got
caught out and then we had to work a little bit harder. But we
didn't work very hard, and we became very close friends. And he
was the one that I had an enormous crush on.

It was a very important relationship; the first sexual relationship, as opposed to emotional, because up until then, although
I'd felt very emotionally attached to him, the lad in boarding
school and perhaps one or two others to a much lesser extent, it
certainly hadn't been the least bit sexual. I mean it just never
crossed my mind. But with this other lad, it was sexual. I think
I'd just turned 14.

From the age of seven, I had so little to do with females. The
boarding school that I went to was all male; the first one I went to
was all male, the second one – there were females, but they were
educated separately and obviously they had their own dormitories,
and we just had nothing to do with them at all. And at that age,
and at that time, boys just didn't want to have anything to do with
girls – they were soppy and silly and all the rest of it. Whereas
today, I suppose even eleven-, twelve-year-olds, are quite interested
in the opposite sex. But it certainly wasn't the case then. So I was
rather afraid of them, I suppose.

But at the same time, looking back, I'm fairly convinced in my
own mind that right from the age of about seven or eight, even
though I didn't think at all in sexual terms, that I was very much
attracted to other boys, and the thought of other girls just then
didn't enter into it. And that continued right the way through to
when I went to the secondary modern school and met Charles.
There were a couple of times when girls would try and attach
themselves to us and I think we – perhaps myself more than him
– didn't really want girls hanging around with us; we preferred our
own company. And certainly from my point of view it was for
sexual reasons. I didn't want girls coming between myself and
Charles. I don't think he felt that way. I think his feelings were
that girls were a bit cissy and that they didn't like the sort of
things we liked doing. But I think right throughout that period I
felt a great affinity towards my own sex. And something which I've

become aware of more in recent years is that men and women smell different. And although I get on very well with them and I'm far from being a misogynist, and I like women, get on well with women, there is something about the smell of women that I find very, very off-putting indeed. And there are times when I find it uncomfortable to be in close proximity to a woman, so I don't know if that's got anything to do with it.

But I think even looking back, there was something about women that put me off a bit. Matron was different because, you know, in boarding school matron is not really seen as a woman, she's something apart. But all other women that I came in contact with seemed, you know, I won't say an alien species exactly, but I had so little to do with them, never got used to them, sort of thing.

Although Charles didn't have the same feelings towards me, I think he had a certain affection for me, so a certain amount of sexual activity did take place after a while. It was more sort of experimentation really, and the sort of thing that probably, looking back on it, he would say, 'Oh well, it was just, you know, a phase I went through.' For me, of course, it was something quite different, but for him, I suspect it was just a phase of interest, and he then went on to have normal heterosexual relationships. But for me, it was certainly quite something.

After school, Charles and I decided to enlist in the army. Unfortunately, he didn't get in and I did. And so I, right from the start, wanted to get back out again, but it's not that easy once you get in. You've got to finish the training. So I think my design was to finish the training and then get out, which I eventually did. But during the course of the training I enjoyed some of it and after I got over Charles, I suppose there were occasions where I felt very close to other people in the army. They were all about the same age as yourself and they were all pretty immature, and we were all sort of locked away from females, so there was a certain amount of emotional activity. There wasn't a lot of sex, even with the one lad that I was very fond of. There was never any sexual activity at all between us. We were just very fond of each other, and on the day that I left he actually kissed me on the cheek, and that was as close as it ever got. But there was a sort of underlying current of emotional relationships going on, not just with myself, but I felt with others as well.

By that time I would be what, 17, 18, yeah I'd be about 18. And then I met someone else. I changed jobs yet again, met someone else; got very, very attached to him and we did fumble about a little bit. It was nothing very much, but I remember taking him home. And I was head-over-heels in love with him and, you know, what I wanted most on earth was to tell my mother, you know, look at this wonderful person, and look how lucky I am that he seems to like me. But looking back on it, I remember sort of fawning all over him. I probably looked ridiculous actually. I remember his feet were cold. It was in the middle of winter and I took his shoes off and sat on his feet and we were on the settee. And I remember my mother giving a bit of a disapproving look; and shortly after that she went round to see his parents, and shortly after that again he was shifted off – went to live with an auntie and uncle somewhere in the Scotland.

I may be wrong, but I convinced myself that it was done because, you know, we were fond of each other – it was no more than that. I mean there was no real sexuality, but it was just that we were working our way towards it. And I think parents right away recognise it; felt very embittered about that, but my mind was taken off it because, at that time, another relative died and I was left some money in this bequest. My mother was left some, but I was actually left a small amount as well. And I decided that what I wanted to do was go to France; enjoyed it very much, but then my mother was taken ill and, I mean, I'd left her in reasonable health. She wasn't happy for me to go, but she was decent, you know, okay. And she wasn't an enormous age, although she was getting on. She was in her late fifties, by then. And so you know, I thought, well I'd better go back. And so I saved up and eventually, I did go back home again. I had roughly a year in France, thoroughly enjoyed it – had a wonderful time; no sexual activity at all, but at that age it didn't seem to matter. Later on it started to matter a lot, but at that age it didn't seem to matter.

After a while, I really started to feel the need to have a relationship with somebody. I'm not quite sure when that happened, but I started a job and a young lad came to the firm looking for work. He was prepared to do anything and so I said, 'I can find you a little job to do.' Well, to cut a long story short, he did one or two jobs round the place. I got to know him, and I got to know his mother. And his mother was very upset because her husband had left her. She'd got these children to bring up, mostly young children. He was the eldest, and in his last year at school. I was a bit older. I wasn't that much older, but I was sort of twenty-one. Although in maturity, I was no older than him in a way, because I was still very shy and sort of retiring. He was about fifteen, fourteen, nearly fifteen. He was still at school. And you know, she said, 'Oh, it's nice of you to take an interest in us', and I said, 'Oh, I enjoy his company.' And it gradually evolved that I became responsible for him, because he wasn't going to school. Well he was going to school, but then he was disappearing, so I used to actually take him to school. So I got to be a bit responsible for him, and I suppose she thought of me as a sort of useful addition to the family. I used to stay there sometimes and a relationship of sorts developed. I mean he didn't want any sexual relationship, but he didn't mind me being affectionate with him and that was about the extent of it.

I wanted to have a sexual relationship with him, but I was realistic enough about him to realise that wasn't possible, and that if I tried that, he would have said, 'No, no, fuck off, that's the end of it', sort of thing. So I just never did approach him in that way, but certainly the desire was there, the wish to have a physical relationship. And I knew him for altogether, I suppose, about five years. By the end of that time it wasn't exactly a sexual relationship, but he would – when he got to be about seventeen, eighteen or something like that – he would come and visit me. And he knew that I was turned on by him so, you know, he'd sort of play up to it a bit and say, 'Go on, you have a go', or something. As soon as I put my arm, he'd sort of, you know, push off, or whatever, but he'd goad me a little bit. I'd sort of spent a bit of money on him from time to time, but he never really developed the way I would have liked him to develop. But at the same time, I suppose, at least there was somebody there to sort of care for, somebody to take an interest in. And he did get into all sorts of scrapes, which I helped him out of. The last time I saw him, he ran away from Borstal and turned up on the doorstep. He stayed the night and I told him in the morning, I said, 'Well, you're going to have to go back'. He said, 'No', he said, 'I'll stay here.' And I said, 'No, you can't stay here', I said, 'because they'll probably come and look for you here. They'll know your mother's address, your mother'll tell them about me and they'll come here and find you.' And so he saw sense and he did go back, and I didn't see him again. So that was the end of that; it was a real shame.

VERNON

Vernon also describes himself as homosexual in sexual orientation. He was aware of this from an early age. However, during his youth, homosexuality was illegal and carried a high degree of social stigma. Thus, Vernon reports that he suppressed his sexuality for many years. This meant increasing frustration, which he links to the offence that led to his imprisonment in middle age. It was clear during interview that Vernon is quite unrepentant and feels no remorse about the acts which led to his incarceration. The transcript presented below reveals that Vernon sees himself as a victim of circumstance and bad luck. He was too old to benefit from the changes in the law and attitudes regarding homosexuality and, indeed, sex in general. In his view, inconsistencies in the laws relating to homosexual and heterosexual sex contributed to his imprisonment.

The point is I'm a homosexual, always have been. I knew this before I was eight or nine years old. Whether I was born that way, or whether it had something to do with my childhood; I have no idea, but I knew then. But of course in those days it was unmentionable; the word 'gay' hadn't even been invented and of course it was totally illegal. And so I had to face the fact that I was going to go through all my life without having any sexual relationships whatsoever; and I accepted that, but as time went on I found I was getting more and more frustrated. I had to find some sort of sexual outlet. It was no good, I just couldn't keep it going; and this came to a head when I came back to Britain to work, just at the time when the law on homosexuality was changed. But it was too late as far as I was concerned, because I was over the top I reckoned – couldn't imagine anybody being interested in me. And then, when the school I taught at went comprehensive, purely by chance, without planning it or intending it, I met this young lad who well, I got interested in. I don't think frankly there was anything sexual to start with, that came later, but I gradually got more and more involved with this kid and he actually wanted to have sex with me. I didn't in fact suggest it to him, that's what mattered.

If I hadn't been a homosexual, I would presumably have been happily married and the temptation wouldn't have come along; if I'd been able to have had a legal sort of relationship when I was young, then the situation wouldn't have arisen. But I couldn't – it was illegal, had to be kept quiet. When you get to the age of about forty things suddenly start to come to a head, you know – 'Gosh, I'm beginning to get old; I haven't lived yet, I'd better do something about this.' This is why middle-aged men take risks that they wouldn't have taken otherwise. And I think there was an element of that in it, frankly, because when the temptation came I didn't really resist it at all. I mean I knew it was illegal, but seemed to think, 'Oh well, what's the harm?' And of course another irony is that half the charges against me would not have been illegal at all if they had been brought just eight weeks later because the law was changed at the time I was up in court and the age of consent was reduced to 18. So there you are, it was just bad luck.

I suspect there are an awful lot of people out there in the same situation as me. And now that the law has been changed, things will improve a bit. I still find it extremely odd that it's illegal to have sex with anybody male under the age of 18, but with girls it's all right at 16. Presumably boys are much more vulnerable than girls and, therefore, they've got to have extra protection.

It also seems very odd, in these days of open sex, where children are actually encouraged to talk about it; nothing is hidden from them. I mean in my day, you just didn't talk about; it was dirty. My parents didn't mention sex to me at all. I remember when my youngest brother was born, when my mother was pregnant; I went to the town with her one day and she told me that she was pregnant, you see. She said that she had a baby inside her and I said, 'Yeah I know that' and I said, 'How did it get there?' and you know, she couldn't tell me, she couldn't say so at all! I had to find out behind the bicycle shed like everybody else, you know. It was pathetic looking back at it now, but I mean people were like that. And it's very strange that now the atmosphere has changed and at least these people are talked about openly. Still the implications of homosexuality are not being faced up to in my opinion, but there we are, that's the way it goes.

DAFYDD

By contrast with our previous three subjects, Dafydd's sexual identity appeared to be firmly heterosexual. Although he had little to say about his own sexual development, he did recall a traumatic childhood experience. Dafydd was one of the two subjects who reported having been sexually abused during childhood. It was not until many years later that, with the aid of a counsellor, he was able to discuss his own sexual victimisation and begin to come to terms with it.

I used to work with her in a little shop; and, well, that was when I was about twelve. She sexually assaulted me and I was really frightened – too frightened to say anything. I mean, I didn't even know what was happening, in that I was very naive.

Looking back on it, there was no intercourse or anything, but it was hands down the front of the trousers and just fear of everything that transpired, because I just didn't know what was happening. And my ejaculation was, weighing this up, it wasn't even physical enough to ejaculate properly – I was very young and just physically not up to it.

But still, I've hidden that for a long time. It wasn't until just over a year ago in counselling ... We had counselling sessions for seven or eight months, I think, once every fortnight, a couple of hours – good, I enjoyed them. And my counsellor, bless him, he was getting very, very close – chinking away at the armour, until he found a way in. And then one day, he said, 'What happened to you many, many years ago?' He came straight out with it and I was dumbstruck. I had to tell somebody – open the gates, let it out, three hours – poured everything out. I cried – it was like sort of being bathed; cleansed, is it? And he said, 'How do you feel? Don't put any macho image up. Don't put up the tough front that you want people to think you are.' And I said, 'I'm so angry.' At that moment I was. I felt angry at Mum for not protecting me, angry at my step-dad, angry at this woman that, you know, did these things to me. Gosh, everything came through me; angry at myself that I didn't have the guts again to come out and say something about it – stop her.

RONNIE

Ronnie recalls being a very timid, sensitive child, who was easily upset, and who tended to worry. He never enjoyed rough games and felt somehow 'different' from an early age. In the 1950s, sex was something of a taboo subject; homosexuality even more so. It was not until he listened to a broadcast on the BBC Home Service at the age of 17, that he began to understand his homosexual orientation. He recollects his first sexual experiences with other school boys. He also recounts his attempt to establish a permanent heterosexual relationship as a mature adult, which eventually floundered on the rocks of his repressed sexual inclination. The break up of this relationship was followed by a long period of isolation, which seems to have owed much to his inability to relate to other adults on a social basis. Paradoxically, he never felt at ease in the company of large numbers of men until his imprisonment, which brought with it a curious sense of release, even happiness.

I was a very timid child, I remember that, there's no doubt about that; very timid child – easily upset in the little things. I always remember that. I used to worry too much. Maybe that part of me is still with me, you know. I've always been a kind of worrier. At that stage it wasn't as controllable as it is today, you know. Obviously as a child I got on with friends, male and female friends. I think I had the tendency – even now, but certainly in those days – once I'd made a number, a small number, I would stick to those, I wouldn't broaden my society, as it were. Maybe, I don't know. But I was never fully at ease from the age of 12, maybe before. I never enjoyed what you can call; what would be understood as the rough boys' games, etc. I felt I was somehow different, from an early age, before I understood what the difference was.

And I remember at one period, even worried myself, 'Am I a cissy?' – you know, that was the big word in those days – and I remember being worried about this, before I fully appreciated any feelings whatsoever; no sexual feelings, but just this pre-knowledge. Because let's face it, back in the 1950s we were very, very innocent compared with today; unbelievably innocent, when you think of it, compared with what people today know about and talk about etc. So even when I went through the secondary school, I didn't enjoy things like soccer and those things. I used to find those very difficult indeed; I wasn't good at them anyway – I was far happier if I could have been left with a book – and I'd find ways of getting out of those things.

But at the same time then – from the point of view of making friends, especially as you got into your teenage years; they were all grammar school people at first – I was into the usual pop music of the time. We used to go to each other's houses, that kind of thing; we used to socialise in that way. But from an early, early age I did realise of course, that I wasn't following my friends in the sense that they were – later than probably today, but 14, 15 – becoming interested in girls and I wasn't. I couldn't understand that, you see, because such a thing as homosexuality was something one never heard about.

It's hard to believe actually that there we were. We were supposed to be grammar school people who read widely and everything, and yet I was 17 before I heard a programme on the radio which actually summed up homosexuality; and I was 17 before I realised where I fitted. Today, this is unbelievable, but this is true of that period, of the 1950s. I remember at the age of 17 hearing this programme – Home Service as it was in those days – absolutely glued to it. Very upset afterwards, by the way, very upset, I remember that; couldn't talk to anybody, because there was nobody in those days you could turn to, to talk to anyway. I suddenly realised that what they had been talking about on that programme was me and I was very upset. I went through a tremendous depression I remember, after it, couldn't talk to anybody, literally nobody. And nowhere could you find more information on homosexuality, which is very strange really. I remember that period very, very well. And I think, quite frankly, that it must have taken me a very, very, very, very long time to get to terms with that feeling, that knowledge. Talk about being in the closet – I was locked in the closet.

It meant that I found I was unable to make relationships with men. I was happy with women. Looking back, I had two or three close men friends, who were friends, nothing more; friends in the true sense of the word, I'd been with them through education. But I was never happy to be in the company of a large number of men. I was very young. That has continued basically, right up until the present day to an extent. And I was worried about this before coming here. What has surprised me being here is how much at ease I am. I'm more at ease now, and have been happier here in the last ten weeks, than I have been for years and years, which is completely ... I can't understand this myself at the moment.

Is it because things have come to light? I don't know, I'm only saying this at the moment. Sometimes you rack your brain trying to think about things. I was very, very, very calm when the trial and everything came to light and even before then. If you'd told me two or three years ago that these things would come to light, I'd have told you then, probably I'd have gone into a state of depression – I'd want to finish everything. I'm amazed how calm I've been, almost glad in a strange way that things have come to light. As I say, I've been happier here than I've been for years. I'm getting on well. It's a male society. And I don't understand why I'm able to. I'm so much at ease with all these different men here. For the first time in my life I'm feeling I'm an equal with them. Not on the sexual basis – that doesn't come into it, we never talk anything of that sort here; that's the lovely thing about this place as well, you know. No-one talks about your past. I don't know, I feel accepted here. It's strange, I haven't quite worked it out yet.

My first sexual experiences took place when I was about fourteen, fifteen. But they were homosexual experiences with one or two of my peers at that period. People who in time went forward to heterosexual relationships. And I remember those. They were basically, as you would say, just boyish things, at that period. But I do remember them. I think possibly they meant more to me than they did to the other people involved. They were just basically mutual masturbation of some sort, nothing more than that, that was it. But I do think that, yes it's a strange phrase to use, but I was going to say that they gave you a taste for something. I was comfortable in those relationships, even at that age, and I honestly felt there was some kind of – I'll use the word in its broad sense – love involved, which I'm positive the other people partaking didn't feel. It was an act to them, but I'm positive that, even at that period, I definitely got comfort from them; there's no doubt about that, and I looked forward to the next one. Now I don't know whether they did, I couldn't say. But I do remember that, at the age of 15, 16 and I remember one at the age of 16, 17 – same age group, if you know what I mean. But from the age of 18 onwards, there was no relationship whatsoever with anybody 'til I was 28.

Much later on, during the period I was teaching in the south, I got into a nonsexual relationship with a woman – we were very close. And we went together, as the term was, for about two-and-a-half years. And I thought I was very, very fond of her; I think her feelings for me were greater than my feelings for her in that way. I couldn't make the ultimate step-over, which would have meant a full sexual relationship, which would be needed for marriage. And I remember finally breaking up, for both our sakes as it were. And that was difficult, but strangely enough it became a relief as well. I think there was always that fear; I knew myself and there was always that embarrassment that I didn't have full sexual inclinations of a normal kind, and the word normal is a very pertinent word there. People today would tell you that I'd used the wrong term, but my feeling at that time was that I was not normal. And maybe once that relationship had gone I didn't have to think much about that kind of thing. I think that was the reason why. I should have been more upset than I was. She was upset; fair enough. She got married within six months of our breaking up. Two years later, after I'd moved back to my own home area after my father's death, to live, she started corresponding. She wrote again, but I didn't reply. She was a married person, even though the marriage wasn't successful.

But that was a kind of key event you see, that breaking up, because I was finally now resigned to the fact that I was not going to get married. I'd played around with the thought before, but I think at that moment I'd finally accepted it.

I always think of my life in the 1960s, 1970s and 1980s in a kind of decade system. The 1960s was spent living away from my home area, in a different environment. In the 1970s I was back in my home area. I found it restrictive. Also, the people you'd been brought up with had moved away. They had moved away, as I had done as a 20-year-old and most of them had not come back. One or two of my previous friends had come back, and I became very close to quite a few of those; I'd visit them, they'd visit me, type of thing. And yet eventually, they moved away as well.

So there was a period when I did become quite isolated and I couldn't, you see – again I'm back to this thing – I could not make good relationships with other adults. There was a rugby club not far from where I lived and people would say, 'You should come up with us' and that kind of thing. I could never let myself go and visit those places, I don't know why. There was always a fear of going into pubs, clubs, places where male-orientated dominated. I don't know the reason for that. I just wasn't at ease. I did end up in those situations, as you did occasionally. I was there a couple of times and I was much happier to be out of there, I don't know the reason for this; it's nothing sexual. I wasn't rejecting those people or looking at people in a sexual manner, or frightened I would be, I just was not at ease in those groups. But the socialising side is something I'm never really good at – mixing socially with people, I don't know why. I'd always be frightened of people. And I remember saying to my doctor before coming here – before the trial I knew I'd end up somewhere like this – 'the place I think I'm frightened most of going into is prison. I'm frightened of being in an environment where I'd be forced to socialise with people.'

When I came in here, you have a chat with your personal officer. The one that I drew was a pretty tough man actually – didn't like him the minute I saw him, didn't like him. I told him my feelings about this and he said what I'd got to do, I'd got to take part in things. Well I've done all this and he was right. So you see, I respected that man. I like him now – somebody I didn't like at first. I thought he was a bit hard. I'm amazed here, how many friends I've made and how I've been accepted; and that I have a feeling that I was always, well, rejected. I don't know why; I wasn't rejected at college; I wasn't rejected amongst my own professional friends.

JAMES

James was the other subject who recollected having been sexually abused as a child. As is clear from the transcript, James feels that there was a direct link between his sexual victimisation as a child

and his own later acts of child sexual abuse. His victimisation gave
him what he terms 'a warped sense of sexuality'. His parents, who
became aware that their son was being sexually abused, later told
him that they too had noted a marked change in his behaviour at
that time.

I think a lot of where all this hoo-ha – where all this business
started, was when I was a child. I was growing up in a very poor
area, and I was very musically-orientated and was chosen at the
age of 11 to sing in a musical. And one of the adults involved –
sorry this is still quite difficult to talk about – one of the adults
involved, he wasn't actually immediately involved, he was more on
the fringes of the group, was using the group for wrong purposes, if
I can put it that way and I myself was abused by him. At the time
– I mean I've sat and thought about this a lot – at the time, I
think I was quite glad of the attention and – not that I didn't have
a good childhood, I had a very good childhood, very supportive
parents – but it was as if I was being singled out as a little bit
special.

But I think right from then, I have had a very warped sense of
sexuality. When I was twenty, I set up house with a woman who
was pregnant by me. We never got married but lived with each
other for quite a few years, right up until I was about twenty-
seven, twenty-eight. But there was nothing in the relationship apart
from the physical.

I've since talked to my parents about what happened when I
was a child and my parents said they didn't actually know, but
they had a very good idea, because quite often they would ask me
very pointed questions, which I would always avoid. And in fact
they got to the stage where they actually found this impossible and
more or less threatened him with the police. He just sort of
laughed at them. I didn't know this at the time this is just, you
know, what I've been told afterwards. And my parents say my
whole personality started changing from round about this time. I
became very secretive and would never speak to anybody about
anything. All my relationships seemed to be on a very superficial
level. From being a sort of bright, lively child, I became very isolated. I just wanted to be on my own and I suddenly withdrew
back into myself – if that's the best way to put it.

I thought I'd found Mrs Right and so we set up home together.
My parents were very against what was going on, but I more or
less said to them, you know, 'It's my life, I'll do what I like. If you
don't like it, well, tough', more or less. But I was chasing some

sort of ideal. My parents were very, very happily married and I think I was desperately looking for that sort of relationship, that bonding – you know, the need to be wanted.

5 EDUCATIONAL AND EMPLOYMENT CAREERS

This chapter focuses on our subjects' educational and employment careers.

Although he did not enjoy or, indeed, do well at school, Kim went on to a successful career and, through his occupation, was invited to undertake voluntary work at a school. Married with four children, he led a double life involving homosexual relationships and child sexual abuse.

Harry, despite his boarding school education, was unable to achieve lasting success in the occupational sphere. He had a succession of different jobs running parallel with a long line of unsatisfactory homosexual relationships. He carried out voluntary work in different settings, which included work with vulnerable children.

Vernon, also a professed homosexual, had a long career as a school teacher, which began with a lengthy spell in Scotland. On his return to England, he held a senior position for many years.

Dafydd was sexually abused as a child. He had a variety of jobs which culminated in his being imprisoned for offences of dishonesty. After discharge from prison he went into youth work. He is married with three children.

Ronnie moved from a working-class childhood to a successful career as a school teacher. In spite of a deep sense of inferiority, which he attributes to a very poor relationship with his father and his own sexuality – Ronnie describes himself as a homosexual – he nevertheless succeeded in attaining the position of deputy head of a primary school.

James was sexually abused as a child, did not like school and was happy to leave at the earliest opportunity. He also married early and later divorced. As seems to be the case with Kim, through his occupation, James was invited to undertake voluntary work with vulnerable children.

Like Ronnie's, David's origins are also decidedly working class.

He too overcame many obstacles in gaining access to a professional occupation in the Church.

When interviewing our subjects, we were particularly interested in the decision making processes that culminated in their obtaining work which gave them access to children. It may be noted that only one of the men – Harry – openly admits that he was initially motivated to work with children because he found them sexually attractive. However, as indicated above, there is also a suggestion that this too may well have applied to both Kim and James. Like Harry, Kim worked with vulnerable children in a voluntary capacity. James too, originally gained access to children through voluntary work, before gaining full-time employment in social work.

We were also seeking to explore the possibility that there may have been factors in the social systems of organisations that somehow aided our subjects in perpetrating child sexual abuse. Thus, David's account is of particular interest in that it serves to highlight how a sub-culture within the established Church contributed to his criminality. It may well be that such sub-cultures exist within other professions.

KIM

On leaving school, Kim left his parents' home to go to college. While at college he met his future wife. During their courtship he maintained homosexual relationships. This seems to have marked the beginning of what appears to have been a rather extraordinary double life. His public face became that of the happily married man who was successful in a respected occupation. This front masked a clandestine life of homosexual relationships and sexual abuse of boys. Kim had planned to emigrate but gave up the idea because his wife had been reluctant to leave England. Consequently, he began a long and successful career in which he reached a high position. However, as will be seen in the transcript which follows, his respected occupation provided direct access to vulnerable youngsters.

I didn't feel totally happy with my home life, although I had what should have been, or to all appearances was, a perfect home – totally caring parents. But I felt that I was not understood at all. Nobody knew about my sexual leanings and Mum's thing was, you know, 'Go out and find yourself a nice girl.'

What I wanted was a nice bloke, you know, but trying to tell your mother that in the 1940s and 1950s was not on, not in those days. My parents would have freaked, and so would most of their friends.

Dad wanted me to come into his office. I didn't want to have any of that. He tried to fix me up to go on the whaling fleet. I didn't want any of that, so I went to college. A young guy there called Michael and I were very fond of each other, and we had quite a relationship going. He was my first true love, if you like, and I've never forgotten him. I'd love to know where he is now.

Anyway, things went on. I moved around various jobs in the south and one of my mates down there talked me into going on a blind date with a couple of girls, and one of those girls is now my wife – really lovely girl. I think the attraction with her was that she was such good fun. She was not sexually demanding in any way; in fact, you know, she was quite happy if nothing occurred, which suited me down to the ground. So I had a very strong relationship with her. Meanwhile I was having a relationship with a bloke as well, which nobody knew anything about. I got into awful trouble with her through being a flirt with the other girls that she was working with, but that was all part of my front.

Because, basically, of parental expectations and peer expectations, I married Diane. I'm glad I did. It's been a very successful marriage. We've been together for thirty-odd years. Now I've got grandchildren. And I think we have given our kids the best that anybody could give them despite my undercover life, which didn't even appear until I was nicked.

Anyway, when I got married I needed a decent income, so I joined the ——. I didn't really know what they did at the time, but it was a job, quite a secure job, so I joined, and got a little house. We got married and we lived there and we've both been very happy. But all the time this was going on, I had a man in the background. The excuses that I used to get out of that house were absolutely amazing. But it continued, and two or three years after I was married I just couldn't hold it together any more, so I kicked this bloke into touch and I went for about six years without a partner at all.

I've been in the —— 30 years. I retired when I got nicked; I only had a couple of months to run. Wonderful life, absolutely wonderful life – very exciting. Made some wonderful friends. I wore many hats as the ——, and so I had a pretty big job. Now I've left, there are three people doing my job. Yep. Yes, it was very stressful in a lot of areas. I felt that I was doing a worthwhile job, most of the time. I have seen some traumatic sights in my time. Apparently people are having counselling now; they didn't then – made jokes about it.

I met some of the lads I was involved with through my job. I was asked to go and visit a special school, many, many years ago. At that time I got interested in climbing and I was an instructor. And the headmaster and me got on to the subject of climbing, naturally, as climbing to me wasn't a sport, it was a disease which I'd caught. He said, 'We've got no-one to take the kids climbing. Would you help?' And I said, 'Yes'.

The school, the climbing, this went on for some years. But the school changed policy and everything and the school packed up, and so ... But climbing seemed to be quite an attraction for all these youngsters; it was like a bloody magnet for them. And a lot of my victims were attracted to me – or I attracted them – I don't know how you want to look at it. With the climbing, it was sport and activities.

Another thing that's being looked at very closely is why I suddenly developed sporting activities when I hated sporting activities as a kid. I suppose the only way I could justify that, was by saying that although I hated sports as a kid I loved the mountains. I loved climbing – the one thing that I really loved and excelled in. My kids were also sort of growing up, they wanted activity. It was a natural progression for my family, which developed outside the family afterwards.

HARRY

On leaving school, Harry joined the forces in order to be with a school friend. However, his friend failed the medical. This dampened his enthusiasm for service life considerably and after completing his basic training he got his mother to buy him out. This episode in his employment career was followed by a succession of different jobs. He also recalls undertaking voluntary work in a large hospital for mentally retarded children. At one point he says the motivation for this was his attraction to young boys. He also relates that his decision to take up voluntary work was conditioned by the disappointment of a failed relationship; that he needed something worthwhile to fill his time and that he enjoyed the affection he received from the children. Later on he recounts how his interest in games facilitated access to disturbed children.

I'm homosexual and I realised that at a fairly early age, and the main reason for wanting to go into the forces was that the boy that I was head-over-heels in love with at school was going to join. So you know, naturally, I wanted to join as well. And it backfired on me because we both took medical examinations and I passed and he didn't. So I found myself in the forces – we were separated anyway. Went in as a cook, quite enjoyed it, but like I said the whole reason for going in was him. So, you know, as soon as I went in I was sort of angling to get back out, which I did after a little while. My mother bought me out, actually, after I completed my training.

It wasn't quite what I ... well, it wasn't at all what I expected. I expected my friend to be there for one thing and I also expected it to be, you know, lots of travel and the rest of it and of course in the first bit it was basic training. And basic training meant you were in the camp all the time, you wouldn't go out at all. Even when you finished that, you'd still got further training to do and it didn't seem as if it was getting anywhere. So I got my mum to buy me out; didn't cost a great deal, just had to sort of pay a sum – I forget how much it was. An aunt had died and left some money, so it wasn't a problem at all. I'd told my mother for some time that I was distressed and she said, 'Well, you know, I can always buy you out if you're sure that's what you want to do'; so I was bought out.

And then I went into various jobs, drifting from one thing to another. Because I had a fairly good education and was reasonably bright, they were mostly jobs with good futures – you know, training managers, things like that. But to be honest, I didn't really knuckle down to them, I didn't have the motivation really. I don't know what I wanted to do quite honestly; I never really sat down with anyone and discussed what I should do. I did work for a while in ... I can't remember the name of the place, but it was a cinema where they occasionally put on shows, so I was a projectionist. But I also used to help when they put on shows there and that of course was very interesting. I enjoyed that, but it was very, very low money. And my mother by that time was sort of living off her savings and money was important.

So I changed. I worked for a store as a trainee manager for a while after that, and later worked for other stores as a trouble-shooter manager. I liked the challenge of that – the responsibility, the fact that I was called in whenever there was a problem. If the manager had sort of been stealing from the company, they would obviously sack him on the spot, so there had to be someone to move in straight away and take over. Or, if there were problems with staff, something of that sort, somebody had to go in, you know, like a new broom and sweep clean – so that was my job. I was very conceited at that age – young man, I thought I knew everything. So that was the sort of thing that I was doing.

They were similar types of job I suppose, but no great consistency. I tended to be a little bit big for my boots. I was doing very well and I felt I should be promoted to area manager. I was only, well I would say, about twenty and really expected to be promoted to area manager. And when I wasn't, I berated the managing director and told him that I could run all three shops in the area where I was working if he paid me two wages. That didn't go down too well. Can understand why now. At the time I thought it was very silly, you know, not to take me up on it. I was very young, very full of myself.

By my late twenties, I started to settle down a little bit more. But even right up until before I was arrested, I was tending to sort of do something for a few years, but the periods were getting longer. I mean, they were getting to be five, six, seven years, instead of a couple of years, or something like that. But there was still the freak tendency to sort of go from one thing to another. And not that many years ago I switched completely from management to working in a park. I fancied working outside and they were absolutely amazed when I applied for the job because they said, 'Well you're a manager of a shop, so what do you want with park work?'... 'Actually', I said, 'your pay structure means I'm getting an increase in pay, if I work as a labourer in the park', and he found that difficult to believe – it was true – and I enjoyed that.

I did a lot of voluntary work as well, different things. This was linked to my offence actually. Because I found I was attracted to young boys, I did some work in a large hospital for mentally retarded children and we used to go there once a week, all day on Sunday, and help out. And I found it very rewarding because the children were very affectionate and, you know, they sort of looked forward to you going there and I found it very rewarding to sort of be wanted in that way. And I'd not really found a relationship so, you know, it was just sort of to be wanted really. But I did one or two other things as well with the elderly, and later on I got a full-time job working with the elderly. But the main thrust of the voluntary work I did was with youngsters, you know, because I had it in the back of my mind that this was the way to get some affection from someone. I did have a relationship for a while – this was during the period when I was still working for one of the stores and going into the period where I was working in the parks department.

I had a steady relationship with a chap I'd known for some time. We set up home together; eventually bought a house and it went very well for a while, until he decided that it wasn't interesting enough just having one partner. He wanted to have two, or three, which didn't go down very well with me. So he left and I was sort of left on my own. So, I had the house and after some time I got fed up with being on my own, sold the house and had a holiday. Hadn't had a holiday for some years, so I thought, 'Well I'll have a really good holiday'; bought a car, toured all round Europe and came back with no money – spent it all within a couple of months. And that brings us almost up to date. Having got back to England, I was looking for a job – any kind of job, preferably one with accommodation. And I was lucky there, I found a job as a caretaker of a large property. I then changed jobs completely. Again, I needed a job which had accommodation, since I'd gone from this place, and so I got a job working for the local authority and that was looking after elderly people. I'd done some of that as laundry work in the past so that qualified me, and I took some training in that and quite enjoyed the job. And I did that for about five years, just over five years, until I was arrested.

The voluntary work sort of came in, as I said, round about the time that I split up with this permanent relationship, because I was sort of feeling – I suppose looking back on it – I was sort of feeling, you know, that I'd been let down, that I needed, wanted, something, you know. And so it fulfilled a dual purpose; it gave me something to do, something worthwhile to do, but also it gave me something in, you know, the affection that I was getting from the children at the hospital and one or two other places. There was an organisation that had a meeting once a month and I used to go along there. I'm very interested in games of all sorts, and I used to take those along and the children took to these, found it fascinating and got very enthusiastic. So I got quite a lift out of that.

VERNON

A life-long bachelor, Vernon read modern languages at university. He chose languages because, when combined with teaching, they provided a passport to virtually anywhere in the world. Thus, his choice of career seems to have been conditioned by a desire to travel. The first part of his teaching career appears to have been interesting and rather exciting. After completing National Service, he spent a considerable number of years working overseas. In middle age, however, he returned to England and spent 20 stressful years as head of languages in a large comprehensive. Worn out and close to breakdown he opted for early retirement. But shortly afterwards his infirm mother came to live with him so that he could look after her. This took the shine off his retirement to such a degree that his imprisonment for an offence that had occurred many years earlier was, for him, a kind of release.

When I was 18, I went to university to read languages, and deliberately chose a university a long way from home so that I could get away. And then after that was National Service, and then after that I got work abroad.

Eventually I came back to Britain because well, you know, I was getting on a bit and it was a choice either of sort of vegetating quietly for the rest of my life or getting back to Britain. I was beginning to miss some things about Britain which I liked, so I came back and got a job in —— where I have been ever since, for the last quarter of a century now.

My university fees were paid by a government grant and one of the conditions I had to sign for was that I would teach for at least two years in a British state school, but they didn't say when – at any time – so I thought, 'That's fine'; so I signed.

The two years' National Service were a complete waste of time and effort. The trouble was that they couldn't do anything with the National Servicemen because all the critical trades required at least a three-year training course and you were only there for two years. And anybody with a degree – unless it was in something like physics or engineering – was shoved in the Education branch. So I found myself posted and there must have been about six or seven of us in the Education branch there. There was absolutely nothing to do. Nothing at all! We used to sit and read magazines all day, by the window. And if we saw a senior officer coming, we would hastily get some papers out and pretend to work, and this went on for months – it was driving us mad!

After that was when I went abroad. When I came back I went to a grammar school; that was the first time I'd ever taught British kids. Though I say British, most of them even in

those days were non-British. It was a Church school, which had
to have a Church of England service every morning but, because
there were so many different communities in the school, they
had to have four other assemblies at the same time – there was
Roman Catholic, there was Muslim, there was Jewish and I
heard something else as well. Anyway, they seemed to think that
I was Jewish, so they said, 'Would you go and help with the
Jewish assemblies?' So I said, 'Yes, I don't mind.' I had already
applied for a job abroad again and I knew I stood a good chance
because I'd already worked for them for two years, but I needed
this as a fill-in. And the day I started work at the school, I got
a letter saying, 'You have been accepted. You will go to ——.
Report there on 1 January.' So the day I arrived at the school, I
went into the Head's office and gave him my resignation; it's the
only time in my career I've seen a headteacher totally at a loss
for words.

I was put in charge of a boarding house with 12 people on
the staff – none of them spoke a word of English. I could tell
you endless stories, but anyway I'd better not. It was a real
experience being at the school; it was a totally different medium,
and it was a time-warp because the school had not changed at
all since Independence. And it was like living in Eton – as it
was a hundred years ago – it was incredible.

But then again, after four years I thought, you know, 'Should
I spend the rest of my life here or should I do something else?'
And I was beginning to get middle-aged by then and thinking,
well, I do miss bacon for breakfast and it would be nice to
actually watch television occasionally, and so on. And so I decided to pack up and come back to Britain, and I got the job, as
I say. I was made Head of Languages and it was quite a challenge, but it was extremely stressful. The stress was there all the
time and you were working from half-past eight in the morning
'til sometimes ten o'clock at night. You would come home, you'd
have to sit down, mark books and prepare lessons. You had
these endless school committees, which used to go on night after
night. I thought at first this was just settling in, but it got
worse and worse. And I stayed there for 20 years. How I stuck
that I do not know, and in the end I realised that I was facing
a nervous breakdown.

Then they came up with this scheme – because the numbers
were dropping – they came up with an early retirement scheme.
I didn't take much notice of it at first. And then I woke up one
morning feeling really rough and I suddenly realised that I was

the oldest person on the staff! And I thought, 'You're a fool, struggling on like this, you no longer enjoy teaching, can't you get out?' And so, within a week, I gave in my resignation and took early retirement.

That was, what, ten years ago? Best thing I ever did. You know, I felt that at last I was beginning to be able to do things that I had never been able to do before. Unfortunately, the complication was that my mother, who was widowed by then, was getting a little bit beyond it. I put her in sheltered housing, just down the road from me, but she got to the point where she wasn't feeding properly and she set the flat on fire twice; it was getting a bit dirty and so I decided she would have to move in with me, as I was the only one of her children who wasn't working. So I sold her flat, got her in with me and found looking after her was a full-time job. I had to do everything for her, even switch the television on. So that took a bit of the shine off retirement.

And then I was charged with this offence which had taken place 25 years ago and got sent here. Far from being in prison, I've found my freedom here. I think prison was how I was living before I came here, but now I've come here I've been able to do things I couldn't do before. So in many ways, I'd rather stay doing things here, which I'm not supposed to do. The thing I'm dreading is being released, because my mother is still there; my sister is coping with her at the moment, but as soon as I'm released my sister is going to pull out and leave me there, which is going to be terrible for me, but I don't see any alternative. So if they say to me, 'Sorry, we're not going to give you parole', I shall say, 'Thank you very much.'

DAFYDD

At 16, having been a victim of sexual abuse, Dafydd returned to England from Australia and embarked on a career in the forces. He served overseas in several war zones. On leaving, he took up a job while continuing to serve in the volunteer reserve. He was the victim of a road accident and suffered serious injuries. Shortly afterwards Dafydd's marriage broke up and some time later he was imprisoned for a nonsexual offence. This led to an interest in youth and community work and he became youth leader at a local centre. Although, as later transcripts will show, this gave him access to his victim, Dafydd's account suggests that his motivation for entering youth work was to offer genuine help to young people in need.

I joined the cadet force to get me away in the summers – away from that summer I was sexually abused. I did well in the cadet force, what they call student militia. And I went away for a ten-week summer camp, which was training; and I really enjoyed that. Then I got in touch with my real father, my natural dad and said, 'Hey, look, you know, when I'm 16 I really want to come home. I don't want to stay in Australia.' There were some things I wanted to stay in Australia for, but I had to come and find my roots. And lo and behold, Dad sent money over, better than that, he sent a boat ticket. So I was released – loosed upon the unsuspecting world. Came back to England and lived with an auntie, until I was old enough to join up.

But obviously from High School I had no qualifications what-soever, no ambition or interest really. So I thought I'd join the forces. I felt safe, if you know what I mean, from the experience that I'd had. I went for six weeks' training; I thought this was great. You know, the Services had the reputation in the very early 1960s for being extremely tough; it wasn't. If you applied your mind to it, you accepted the discipline as your self-disci-pline as well, it was real fun, it was really good. And I got in with some good guys, real nice guys. And we vowed that we'd stay together – we'd stick together.

And after we'd done our six weeks' training and then went for a further six weeks' driver training, they had these recruiting guys come round. A whole week of either sea transport, or air despatch, or parachute training. And all these wonderful things you can now sort of specialise in. We all joined up for airborne, every one of us, you know, a further twelve weeks then, doing crazy things like jumping out of airplanes – you know, real macho stuff; it was good fun. I was young, eager, fit. I went to —— for six weeks and on the way back from —— landed at ——, and we were told that there were volunteers required for —— for a two-year posting. We put in for that – all of us – boom! Straight down to ——. And we spent two-and-a-half years in ——. Lovely time; I found that I had a real interest in peo-ple, native people. I loved the simplicity of their life, the simplic-ity of their language. I found I had a penchant for languages – I spoke quite fluently.

And my idea of leave was just to go out into the bush and live native. Wonderful – what an experience. I mean the basic, the simple things in life; you love, you learn to love. And the skills of these people, I mean, it just still knocks me back now. You see the —— with their small axes, chipping the edges off a piece of wood and then you get an antelope or a deer, or a giraffe, you know, just magically appears – amazing. I love that, I loved it.

From there, when —— got its independence, went to —— to serve out the three years – a lot of trouble there. Saw my first real violent death there when I was asked to go out in a coach of schoolchildren. The schoolchildren had just got off the bus and we had driven about a mile up the road and there was a traffic jam, an ambush, on what they call the Murder Mile; no whites allowed. And it was a trap laid for us, for the bus. And one of the dissidents had thrown a parcel under the back of the bus and the fuse had already been lit – the silly blighter, as he blew himself and the back of the bus off. All it was, was a pink mist and I was covered in yuck, you know. The body just vaporised, there wasn't a piece of body, just this sticky goo. And I thought 'Yuck!' I'm still shaking a bit now, just thinking about that.

I left —— when my three years was up – came back to the UK. Got a promotion and then was told that the situation in —— was hotting up a bit and they needed experienced men out there, so obviously I volunteered. It was for a six-month posting, but I ended up out there for four-and-a-half years. Again I fell in love with the people. The —— are again very, very basic; in their villages there is just one big, long, house. Amazing. All in one happy community. I've always loved that idea – being next door to auntie, within five minutes of anyone, you know. And I just love that sort of life. And you know you can wake up in the morning and not have to bother about breakfast because it's growing right outside your front door, your pineapple and grapes.

It was very difficult in —— because the enemy was also quite professional. I killed my first man, directly, face-to-face, there. And that's something that's very personal to me. We were under orders, we could see that they were trying to keep the people Communist. Anyway, we laid an ambush and these chaps came across the border and they never went back – we killed them all. That had a very profound effect on me.

I came back to the UK and was almost immediately again sent abroad to ——. This was because —— had just been overthrown by some pipsqueak sort. You know the trouble we had there; had a few fun and games out there, and then came back to the UK. And I had the option of discharge, of leaving the Services, or carrying on for a further nine years. The day I was to make the decision I was told, 'You're going to Northern Ireland.' It just really dried up like that and I thought it was decision time. All of us went down to the Club and decided, 'No', we'd had enough. There are certain things that one has to do when one feels that it's right, and I felt it was right to leave the army; they didn't have to prompt me. I didn't agree with the situation in Northern Ireland – I still don't now, I think we're wrong – but that's beside the point, they're my thoughts. You know, sometimes I can be quite outspoken.

So I went to the Commanding Officer and I said that I wished to be discharged. I didn't want any further duties. So he said, 'Okay, fair enough, what do you want to do when you go out?' So I said, 'Well, I've already made arrangements to do a management course with them.' And he said, 'Well you've got three months to work for ——. See if you like it or not, as a sort of breathing space. If you like it then you stay with them. If you don't, then you come back to us and we'll find you something else.'

Very good the pre-release mechanism in the Services in those days. Now it's just, 'Here's the door – cheerio; hand your kit in on the way out.' I stayed with —— for ten years, six months, during which time, after six months in ——, I didn't miss Service life. But then again it was in an all-male environment – I enjoyed that. And I'd always fancied the Navy. Crazy! So I joined the reserve. And because of something I'd picked up in —— which left my face all sort of scabby my own doctor said, 'Why don't you work here? It will probably clear up in time.' So I did – I stopped going.

I went down to the docks and I joined up as a clearance diver, again working with explosives, where things could go bang and, you know, destroy things. And I got on very well, working two nights a week – 'cos as a reservist you only had to do two evenings a week, and you were off weekends with a fortnight's holiday a year, working holiday.

I was a Branch Manager and we were very short-manned one day; I was called in to do a bullion run to —— early one morning and the road was very icy. The truck in which I was travelling; four of us were travelling in it, went into a skid and we hit the barrier of a bridge. All the coin and all the bags of money slid forward on the floor and tipped the balance and we crashed – schwoo! – straight over the bridge, to the road below and I was trapped in the back. I suffered quite severe head, back and leg injuries; broken left leg, broken right leg, broken right ankle, and the right ankle had completely come adrift and it was just wobbling about on a piece of sinew!

I spent six months in hospital and had the ankle rebuilt. It's not too bad now, but there is some lack of movement. So it left me disabled and sort of bitter, I suppose; quite bitter. I was married with a child and all the money I had in compensation I gave to my wife and set her up in business, while I carried on working. I went back to ——. Unfortunately, I had to be discharged from the Navy reserve as I couldn't carry out my duties properly. I was attached to guns and you have to move very, very quickly. Even on exercise, you have to move very quickly. And I admitted to myself that I wasn't up to it any more. I wasn't getting any younger at all, so I took a desk job on communications which again I enjoyed.

I know it was my fault. I found it very difficult communicating my feelings. It was very traumatic. The whole accident was very traumatic and I hadn't sought the help that I now know that I needed. I caught my wife in bed with a bloke – it was a bit of a surprise. And by trying to save the marriage – going way over the top; a very emotional time – I lost everything, except the baby; lost my home, lost the business, lost everything.

So I moved out, got myself a little bedsit. Obviously I had to start rebuilding my life for myself and my son, for when he grew up. It didn't work out. I left —— and tried carrying on in my own business. The money was good, but the hours were really crazy; seven nights a week, doing —— which left very little time really for my son. I met a young lady, who is my wife now. And she was besotted with me as much as I was besotted with her. Not a worldly girl; a very homely girl. And I had a long, long period where I was afraid to take decisions, to make the decision, you know, that I wanted to devote my life to her, rebuild my family, rebuild relationships.

And I was very distant. I've only got one, sorry three, very close friends that I would speak to about my problems. I'd laugh and joke with people – it's one of the defence mechanisms that I think I've got. In the face of all the adversity that I've seen and had to live in, I've managed to hone it finely – fine tune this mechanism, where you can turn tragedy into humour, you know, and laugh about it. One of my friends – still a very close friend – he'd just left ——, again quite disgruntled; they were not very good employers, but that doesn't excuse what we did.

We actually planned a job. We gave the money back; we gave ourselves up. Got two-and-a-half years, served a year for it.

My girlfriend was waiting for me and I thought, 'Hey', you know. I asked her, 'Will you marry me?' and she said, 'Yes'. So I asked her mum and they were ecstatic, ecstatic. So I got married just after I got out of prison. I worked for 18 months for ——.

One of the things that I was really surprised at, not surprised, I was really hurt at the young men who I saw in prison that looked up to people like me – ex-serviceman. And I thought 'Oh. Oh God! These guys are wasting their lives. I'm wasting my life. I've wasted my life. And these guys are doing the same thing!' And for good reasons or bad reasons – I'm not really too sure of the reasons – I actually signed up as a Social Services volunteer in Manchester. The Senior Social Worker at my local place said, 'Look, we've got an MSc vacancy here, which I think would be ideal. You study psychology and sociology for one year to get your feet under the table and help us out.' So I did. And I was put in with a guy who was the juvenile expert. I found my little niche working with juvenile delinquents – could be my service training, it stood me in good stead.

We set up what we call a trek team – outdoor pursuits, abseiling; taking young lads out and bouncing them off the side of a mountain; giving them a day out; feeding them on worm omelettes and woodlice, you know. They loved it. It was great. When the time came to leave, I took training with the county. It was only two years for Youth and Community Work. And I took over a dilapidated building – it was an old boys' club – terrible place; the kids smashed the windows just for kicks. The leaders would lock themselves in the canteen, pull the shutters down and just let the kids get on with it. I went in there one night and couldn't find any adults at all. And there were kids dancing on the snooker table. And I thought, 'Whoah! Hey, who's in charge here?' 'Well, effing Dave innit, in there.' So I sort of rapped on the door, and someone shouted, 'Go away!' So I walked in and there's these blokes with, you know, bottles and I said, 'Hey, you know, I've just come down to see if I can help, as a volunteer, you know.' 'Well yeah, yeah, go out and look after that lot. Cheerio.' And they slammed the door.

I thought, 'No, this ain't right. This ain't right.' So I went back in, introduced myself, sat down with them for a few minutes and I said, 'Look, you can't let kids get away with this sort of thing. You lead them, they don't run the place. You have to facilitate for them.' They didn't think it could be done and said, 'Oh, this lot are from council estates, like, concrete jungle and all this', you know. Anyway, they resigned after I proved that it could be done.

I went to a bank which was refurbishing and said, 'I want 3,000 yard-square or metre-square carpet tiles, if you're throwing away.' Anyway, the top and bottom of it was, they gave it to us. About £8,000 worth, I think. They gave it to us, just wrote it off. I wrote to Dulux, because they do a community project every year. The most worthy one gets all the paint that they require. So I said, 'Right, I want 60 gallons of floor paint and 400 gallons of masonry paint to do the whole club – inside, outside, the lot; so many gallons of red paint, so many gallons of white – everything.' And I said what I would do during the summer months was get all the unemployed dads down here – and the mums. The Social Services would supply food; we'd get so much off the Social Security for a Community Project; the dads would be employed and the kids would at least get a holiday. It worked – we got the lot. About £18,000 worth of paint. We painted everything – chairs, seats, the lot.

The boys' club was living; it was really thriving with all the equipment. People started taking notice of the club because it was a beautiful, posh, club. We had furnishers give us brand new semi-circular settees, easy chairs – loads of stuff. And it was just great – very well done. I was leading a team, by then – myself and five others. I promoted one of the young lads who was a boisterous little lout, and who turned out to be just the ideal sort to convey the messages that we were trying to get across. We had drugs projects running, counselling working for anyone – lads with problems, parents having problems, you know, with their lads. We used to actually make programmes and it was really good.

RONNIE

Ronnie followed a long tradition whereby bright working-class boys from his area went into teaching. In this he was encouraged by his mother, by his school, by everyone he was associated with, except for his father who seems to have done all in his power to discourage his son. In Ronnie's view, his poor relationship with his father, coupled with his homosexuality, meant that he suffered from an inferiority complex throughout his childhood and adolescence. He

achieved success in the teaching profession and this appears to
have increased his self-confidence somewhat. Ronnie states that he
did not enter the teaching profession because he was sexually at-
tracted to children.

We were under a very strong influence back in the 1950s to go
into teaching. I think in our small rural grammar school, if I'm
right we only had 140 people. You'd have found that possibly
80, even 90 per cent of the people ended up in teaching – it
was the thing in the 1950s. So you see, you were following a
tradition; you had the influence at home. My parents were ordinary working-class people. Although they felt themselves classless,
they were nevertheless working-class people. My mother wanted
me to have a better chance in life than she'd had. She used to
tell me that had my father been the same man she'd married
before the war, he would have felt the same. I don't know what
went wrong. I've never been able to analyse that.

So the idea of going in for teaching was something that my
mother was very keen on. The school was keen on it; she was
keen on it; all my friends were going into the same profession.
Five or six of us went to the college at the same time, from the
same school. So you see, you were following a trend and you
didn't think much else. You didn't think much wider. I did at
one time think of the bank. That was a very, very, very fleeting
idea. So from the age of 14, 15, you were working towards that.
We knew, early on, what we were going to do. The two things
on offer were teaching and the bank. But I followed my way into
teaching and, as I say, there was no alternative. There must
have been alternatives, but it all seemed to be cut and dried
from a very early age, and you didn't argue against it; you went
along with it; no regrets in that sense.

The two years at teacher training college were very, very
happy. I think I was very, very happy in many ways. I was away
from home; I missed home, to say I didn't would be stupid, I
did miss it. I remember being very, very homesick when first I
went away, even though I'd only travelled 50 miles. In those
days 50 miles was far further than 50 miles today. I remember
being very homesick. But I liked the closed life of the college I
was at. It was a mixed college, but it was completely separated
compared with what they are today. We'd work together, of
course, in association times and in lectures – sexes mixed then.
But once a certain time came, we were separate. And I must say
I was very, very happy. Those years were very, very happy. I

made many friends in those years and I was very, very saddened to leave.

I ended up teaching in —— and I always remember a real feeling of homesickness for the college when I got to ——, which is a strange thing to say. But I think I'd been well treated in college, you see. You're treated with everybody else as equals. So I thought, perhaps for the first time, that I wasn't ... I don't know what it is – I've always had this inferiority complex. I know that's in there; something I've had to fight against in my life, to push myself forward. In college I remember the idea of reading in front of everybody used to give me nightmares, 'til you had to do it and once you'd done it you realised it wasn't so bad, you know, that kind of thing.

Once again, I had no confidence in myself. I know as a youngster, and this may sound stupid but it's true, I didn't like myself. When I say I didn't like myself, I don't mean the deep-down personality. I didn't like myself. I was very much aware that I had buck-teeth at one period. I remember that. And I always used to feel that I was worse than everybody else. I don't know why, but I always used to feel that I'm not as good as other people. And it took me well into my twenties before I was able to put that right. I – if you like to reason about this, this nonsense; I remember doing that, reasoning with myself, to bring it out – I always had a dreadful inferiority complex and felt I wasn't as good as other people; I used to believe that strongly. And my mother used to try and tell me that I was, to try and bring me round – my aunt especially also, and my uncle too. But for some reason I didn't like myself at all. I used to think I was ugly, you know, teenagers do often think this, I know that. But I remember it getting to a state, at one time, of deep depression at the age of 14, 15, 16, around there, simply because of that feeling. I couldn't talk to anybody about that.

Looking back now, I can see patterns of behaviour in myself and feelings, which I'm positive if they happened to a younger generation today, they could go and talk about to somebody. The 1950s were the 1950s. Until I was 17, 18, nobody talked about homosexuality. You didn't have people in those days using words like 'queer', those derogatory remarks about you which would have made you feel worse still – didn't have those because the general knowledge of homosexuality was so limited. People were ignorant, simple as that. So it wasn't that I was picked upon because of it. It was a feeling you had inside you. You knew you were different. And for a long time, until this broadcast that I heard on the BBC, I felt that I was the only person. I remember feeling I wasn't quite all there and believing that, by the way, that I wasn't quite all there. And the fact that my father always, every week, week after week after week, ran me down. He never ever said anything to my face, but there was only a wooden partition – what we used to call wainscoting – between us. So it might as well not have been there. I was able to hear everything he said. And I don't know, was it a combination of things? I couldn't tell you really.

The only thing I was good at was academic work. But he said that I was wasting my time at school, that's the feeling. He never ever looked at a schoolbook in his life. And I suppose, basically, that was the one thing I knew I was good at and liked doing and had praise from the staff in school and things because of that. That was the one thing I think I wanted more than anything; for him to just pick up a book, and say, 'That's good. You've done some nice work here.'

I remember the day, the August, when my O level results came out. I was 16 now, not a child, small child, any more. I did have very good results. I was delighted of course. People on the streets – because in those days, of course, they just published in the local paper – everyone knew; they would be congratulating you. He never even asked what I'd got, until a neighbour came in. I remember so well, the neighbour said, 'He has done well, hasn't he?' and he said, 'Oh yes, he has done well' and I know he didn't even know what I'd had. And I remember that hurt at that period. I went back and I remember sitting in my aunt's house and crying at sixteen-and-a-half, crying. And she said, 'It doesn't matter. We all care', I remember her saying that, 'We all care, it doesn't matter.' And I said, 'I'm not going back to school in September' – all these kinds of feelings coming out – 'I want to go away', and all the rest.

My aunt was always an intermediary and she used to say, 'Look, your mother wants you to go, you must do it.' I had to do it for her. And it worked; it worked because I wanted to do these things as well. I wanted to go back. And when I got into adulthood, you see, I wanted to confront him. And she used to beg me, 'Don't, I have to live with him afterwards.' So right up to his death, I never did confront him. And once he died, I think I did regret that. I should have confronted him in a calm way, maybe got to know him. It still hurts today that I never got to know him. He died so suddenly. Even though I was glad at the time, if only I could have got to know him, but I didn't

– it still hurts now. I'm feeling it at this very moment, strangely enough – there we are. After all these years, I'm 55 and it hurts. It doesn't make sense.

I think key events were going to college, leaving college, having a job, starting to teach. These were all basically key events. And also finding, when the time came, that I was good at what I was doing. And I think that gave me the biggest confidence of anything that I'd ever had – the fact that I was told that I was good at what I was doing. You felt you were good, but that's not the point, that's not good enough, you have to be told.

And I remember we had a wonderful headmaster. I was 20, 21 and he was, let's see about my age now, mid-fifties, you know what I mean, an old man if you like. And there were three of us from college who started at his school. He was a father figure to us. He was marvellous. He gave us advice and we could take advice. We could take criticism and everything, and I stayed with him for nine years. In the meantime we had a brand new building and had all kinds of new ways to learn and what-have-you. And through being good in my work, I definitely gained confidence. I suppose in a way, began to like myself a bit more. But in that sense, it was a key factor that I landed in a good place to work.

I definitely did not go into teaching because I was sexually attracted to children. I never looked upon children sexually. I wasn't attracted to them. And as I say, throughout the period I taught away in —— right up, I never used that broad term 'fancied', you know. This is something I talked about with the psychiatrist, when he was saying that I had the tendencies of a paedophile. And I was never aware that I was sexually aroused by children, or pupils to put it like that. So I definitely didn't drift into teaching with anything of that sort, because as I say you followed from old in that period. You didn't really make up your own mind, you could almost say. You didn't disagree with it, you accepted it. I've never regretted it, you know. I know some people who did exactly what I did and had regretted it before they left teacher training college. And certainly in those first few years of teaching, quite a few of those people would drift away and they'd say, 'This is not for me.' Well, on the contrary, I found it rewarding and I found I was good at it. And when you find that you're good at something, it's an extra bonus. But no, I can honestly say that there was no lure of children involved in that sense.

JAMES

James, who was sexually abused as a child, left school as soon as he could. He set up his own business. His career as a child care worker seems to have commenced somewhat by chance, when he visited a special school through his business. James's recollection of this bears some similarity to Kim's account of how he gained access to vulnerable children. How James used his position, and subsequent appointments, to abuse children is covered in the next chapter. Here we can also note that his first job in residential work appears to have placed further strain on an already problematic marriage.

When I first left school. Well, I walked out of school; I'd just had enough. I thought everybody was trying to stare through me as a child. So I sort of thought at the time that I'm not going to do this. I thought, I'm an adult, I'm not a child. I was never a ... I was an adult.

I was 16. Actually, I was not quite 16. I was 15 and school was for children. I just walked out, got myself a job in a shop. Money was very tight, very tight. I didn't really enjoy the job, which I think put more pressure on me. Eventually, I started my own business before I went to college. And for a little while things started to pick up. Business was quite good. But I still wasn't particularly satisfied with my life. There was something desperately missing.

Then I happened to go to a special school in —— to do some repairs. And of course you know what it's like when somebody new comes in, all the kids are there and they stare. Well, I spent a couple of days there and on the last day the Head of Care came to me and said, 'We've watched you since you've been here and you seem to have quite a good rapport with these children. We're always looking for part-time staff to help at weekends, evenings. Would you be interested?' So after a lot of humming and hawing I decided to do it, and I was there about five months on a contract basis. And then I was approached and they said, 'Well look, we've got a full-time job vacancy here. Would you be interested?' And I said, 'Well actually, I couldn't possibly. I've got no qualifications.' He said, 'No, we're not interested in taking qualifications. You've worked here with the children. You get on very well with them. You're quite firm with them, but fair with them. They seem to get on well with you. I can't put it any blunter, but if you apply you'll get the job.'

I went home and talked about it with my wife. She was dead against it. But I went ahead and did it because financially it was a lot better money, you know. But as a result it put even more of a strain on the relationship. Things by this time were pretty rocky – the end of the relationship – and I started spending a hell of a lot of my time at the school. I would offer to do anybody's sleep-ins, or if somebody was off sick, I stood in for them, which of course made the relationship at home even worse, because I can see in her mind I was never there.

Carol, our daughter, would spend a hell of a lot of time at the school with me. I didn't mind; in fact I quite encouraged anybody that had children to bring them in, because it was good for the other children. And the two of us began to see less and less and less of my wife, which I think – I don't think, I know – she felt very bitter about.

DAVID

Despite lacking support at home, David set about achieving his ambition for a career in the Church with considerable determination. He calculated the individual steps towards his goal and attained each in turn. On the advice of his school teachers he completed a teacher training course before embarking on his theological degree. At the end of a long, hard road he was ordained. David talks about the link between the culture of his chosen profession or vocation and the sexual abuse of children by members of the clergy, including himself and a number of his immediate colleagues. He refers to a sub-culture of child molesters within the Church. He further states that there seems to be something within the social system of the Church that encourages child sexual abuse, which gives 'permission' to clergy to commit such acts. He argues that the Church has failed to address the problem because such a course would place a fair number of those who occupy senior positions in a vulnerable situation. He admits to having had sexual fantasies about boys in his late teens or early twenties. But he suppressed these because they transgressed the mores and norms of his working-class culture. In his view, the norms of a certain sub-culture within the Church were altogether different in that they appeared to encourage abuse. He recalls his own self-deception in seeking help from senior colleagues who he also knew to be abusers. What he was really seeking was 'permission' to continue his

*activities. He refers to his sense of guilt, shame and betrayal as
an abuser.*

I decided at 13 that if I wanted to go to university then I would
have to have a language, I would have to have maths, I would
have to have English, I would have to have subjects which would
be acceptable to a university, which would be five years hence
really – if I could get them. At that age, I remember constantly
having in my mind where I wanted to be and what I wanted to
do, and the steps I'd have to make. I remember as a youngster
of about 14 actually, drawing up a little chart of years – 14, 15,
16, 17, 18, 19, 20 – and where I'd be at which time, and
naming myself at those times. And it was on the back of my
wardrobe door until last year, when I moved out and tore it off,
done up 'til I was about 24. And I actually achieved those goals.

One was to – they were stupid things now, looking back, in a
sense – to get from B stream to A stream, from A stream to the
top five; to get O levels, to get A levels, to get to university and to
get ordained; to do parish and on from that. They were small goals
and aims which gave me a direction, really, that I felt gave me
something to channel my quite, quite strong life-force towards.
Quite a positive drive then, within myself, to achieve what I feel I
need to achieve.

At the end of school I did my A level period, and was looking
at what I was going to do, and there was quite a lot of pressure
within the school system to try something else, rather than 'Go
into the Church', as they put it then. But my commitment to my
faith had grown over the years, and I felt this was what I wanted
to do; and this was where I felt I was going to fulfil myself best,
and I decided to go that way and offer myself broader conditions
and be trained along those lines. There were other alternatives,
which never appealed to me, really. So I decided to go down that
road. But then, being fairly young, the system at the time suggested that you go away and train as something else first, so I
went away and trained as a teacher.

I found some of the happiest years of my life training as a
teacher. But all the way along, I had the guidance of the authorities – the Church authorities – aiming towards ordination
and seeing this as a way of benefiting in future work. I spent
four years doing that and had the most wonderful four years, I
suppose, of my life – being with contemporaries, being in a
situation where I could live, grow, develop in relationships. And
I felt it a very creative period. And from there, to go on and do

another degree in Theology, which I found hard going, because they strictly limited you to two years and it was hard academic work – pressurised even to get it done. But again, it was good; it was challenging. And then being ordained. The phenomenal sort of completion of all those years of preparation. Seven years' hard work before you passed. Then going to work in parish and finding it exactly what you wanted it to be, and being very happy and very content within your work to the extent that I really felt that this is exactly what I should be doing. And you wake in the morning – it's a silly sort of idea – but you wake up there feeling quite happy to be doing your work, which I feel is quite a good way of viewing it.

I would think there is a certain degree of sub-culture within the Church, as within any society, and the Church does tend to form itself into a very close-knit society with this nature. I think there is a certain degree of inculturalisation between people who are abusers. I think that to a certain degree you pick up sounds and you pick up, well, ideas and I think you just ... There is definitely, I would think, a culture within the Church. It has a great deal to do, I think, with the fact that there are a lot of single clergy, a lot of clergy who are living on their own, in a situation where they can abuse. But they are not necessarily single clergy, because the first person I went to for help was a married man. There seems to be something within the system which encourages, if that's the word, almost gives permission for others to do it and get away with it. Therefore, you think, 'why won't I?' And I think that's a great mistake and I think the Church has a responsibility for my offending and other people's offending, by not addressing what is a known problem.

There is nowhere to go to. There is no-one to speak to in confidence. There's no system of help set up. It's almost acknowledged by a nod and a wink, but no official action was ever taken. I know it's often very difficult to act on rumour, but it's very easy within the Church to act on rumour because it's a disciplined organisation and you can just pull somebody out and say, 'Hey look, this isn't looking too good. What's going on?' There's none of that ever done. There's no challenging of people's behaviour. I think this is due to the fact that quite a lot of senior management would be people who might feel themselves vulnerable to this. The second person I went to for help was a very senior person who was really more vulnerable than I was, and who has since been arrested as a result. But he wasn't imprisoned because of his position.

I wish I could say I went to them because I wanted them to stop me. But I think, being completely honest, I was really seeking 'permission' to go ahead. I knew it was wrong, but I also felt the need to abuse. There was obviously a need to abuse, otherwise I wouldn't have abused. I had fantasy fuelling fantasy; being in a situation where you can fuel your fantasy. I just wanted somebody to tip me over the edge so that I could then almost give myself an alibi – 'It wasn't my fault, they told me it was okay.'

And again, I think there was a great – I can't speak for others – but I think there was a huge need in me to share the blame, guilt, shame. I just felt it was so wrong that I just had to share it out. And of course there is that huge, huge stigma word. If you get caught, it's illegal, it's wrong, you go to prison. And you almost had to go and cheat on others who you felt were doing that, to say, 'Sir, they aren't getting caught.' Self-preservation.

I'd been aware of those aspects of the culture of the Church since theological college, amongst sixty or seventy other people who were training for priesthood. It's there that you learn the culture, spending three years amongst people who are all going to the same work. And there, I think, was the first exposure I had to this sub-culture. But at that point I felt very strongly and very violently, emotionally, against this culture; and until I actually abused, still felt very strongly against this culture. And after I abused, that increased the guilt, the shame and the betrayal.

I'd not only betrayed myself, my beliefs, but everything. Everything I'd stood against I'd suddenly become part of, and I hated myself and I hated man and I hated everybody that I'd talked to. And I felt also a certain degree – again, it's not an excuse – but you felt almost a certain degree of, 'Damn, it's got to me.' It's like an infection. You feel you are part of it now and the sub-culture consumes you as well. It's like an amoeba, swallowing you too. You suddenly were included within that sub-culture. And you came to be in a powerless situation. Well, it wasn't a powerless situation, but you convinced yourself that you were powerless to do anything about it. 'I'm in it now. I have made this decision. I can't go back.' And therefore you remain within that sub-culture, because you are then on a fear thing, you know – 'Oh I can't step out in case. I can't self-destruct.' I wish I had done so earlier, but it's not a natural thing to do – to put your hands up and say, 'Arrest me!'

I'd had fantasies of abusive situations, but would always throw them out by saying to myself, 'It's wrong. I don't want to cope with that. I don't want that. It's wrong.' These fantasies began in my late teens, early twenties, perhaps. But I rejected them because of my background and culture. The fantasies were kept in check, controlled, by the pressures of the culture that I'd been brought up in. When I changed cultures from a working-class culture, into a middle-class, professional culture, there was a sudden cut-off. All those values had been devalued. Suddenly the working-class values that had been my core were no longer there. I had new middle-class values, and unfortunately I was learning them from the sub-culture I found myself in. And that sub-culture within my new world was contributing to my sexual fantasies.

I rejected my fantasies because they were wrong according to the values and the morality of the Christian Church. And so I felt strengthened by that ability to say, 'Stop. This is wrong.' And I would forcibly, if they were young, sort of stand my corner and say, 'This is wrong. We shouldn't allow this to happen.' But at the same time, I didn't think it was wrong or unacceptable for some-body training for the priesthood to have these thoughts, because others were doing it. Again, you see, it confirms within you, 'Oh well, I'm just like everybody else.' The sub-culture provided me with my answers, basically.

6 HOW ABUSE WAS PERPETRATED

Introduction

The theoretical perspective of Finkelhor (1984) outlined in Chapter 2 creates clear expectations of what our subjects will say when asked about their offending. It will be no surprise if, through their stories, they reconstruct both the context of their relationship with their victims and the relationship itself.

We know that perpetrators will have overcome their own inhibitions to abuse; gained access to potential victims; created and planned opportunities for abuse and 'groomed' their victims with subtlety and care. We also know that in this process they will have abused power and trust through coercion, violence or inducement and exploited the child's innocence and lack of confidence. We can also safely assume that these activities will have taken place within what Finkelhor describes as an 'offence cycle', involving trigger, fantasy, plan, target and opportunity.

Whilst they are not necessarily representative, our subjects' responses reveal plenty of illustrations of these phenomena, but they are interesting because of the detailed content and because they are not responses to specific questions about how and why they offended. Rather, the responses place their offending within the broader social and cultural context and touch on those sociological variables – such as attitudes to women and children, and definitions of masculinity – that affect whether an individual abuses or not.

The following extracts are grouped under several headings that broadly categorise the content, but there is inevitable overlap and blurring of distinctions.

Redefining Relationships

KIM

Confusion is a recurring theme of this description of the relationships involved in Kim's offending. There is an awareness of

*being motivated to pick easy targets, an acknowledgement of harm,
juxtaposed to a restructuring of the relationship of offender to victim into child to child, based on equal power, fun and love.*

The kids were starting to get to school age and youngsters were
coming around from various families, as they do, and I started getting
involved with youngsters, you know. Ten – ten years old, upwards.
And I started forming relationships with them. Now the relationships
I formed were, again, they were youngsters from less fortunate families. As I know now, ideal victims if you like. They were easy to get
at and they liked my lifestyle. It seems that I put myself ..., or
switched my mind back to my schooldays and when I was with these
kids; I was a kid, totally and completely and I was just re-enacting
with them, what I was doing when I was at school. And to me I
could see absolutely nothing wrong in it at all. I had no feeling of
guilt, shame, or anything else, it was just sheer affection for these
kids and good fun. And with them coming back for more, basically, it
just continued.

Some of these lads, I had relationships with for nearly 20 years
and some of them even stayed in contact with me when I came into
prison. And I kicked them into touch – I had to. But that was the
sort of depth of relationship that we had, for whatever reason. You
know, I've been told that it's wrong and it shouldn't be, but that's
how it was. And in my mind, there was no shadow of doubt about
the affection that I felt for these lads; there was no other word for it –
I loved them, whichever way you like to put that.

I really don't know where to go from there. It's very difficult
now for me, to talk, because you wanted first-hand how I felt at
that time, rather than how I feel at this moment in time. There's
a conflict of feelings now, because, you know, I've sort of come to
realise what the hell was going on and switched it all round, and
now you're asking me for my initial feelings of how I felt then and
quite honestly I'm a very confused man.

Yeah. Up until I knocked my, sort of, equal partner on the
head, when I was about 24, to this present time, I have had people
much younger than myself. When I came to prison my two main
boyfriends were in their early thirties and those relationships had
developed since they were about 12, 13 years old. That has now
been cut and I have got to re-establish relationships with adults
roughly in my peer group. I'm finding myself being attracted to the
30-odd-year-old people, which is quite strange. It's probably the
mind playing tricks on me, wishing that I had those partners back
again, that's probably what it is. So I'm having great difficulty

ignoring the 35-year-olds and getting to the 40-, 50-year-old mark –
although I have got a couple of guys in their fifties who I am more
than friendly with at this point in time, so I think I'm managing
to achieve that.

There is no shortage of sexual interest either, in these older
guys. But I still find my mind drifting back to the 35-year-olds. I'm
not, in my own mind, I'm not looking or interested in the younger
element. And I've been out on home leave nine times now. I've
been in the company, or in areas where youngsters are around. I'm
not sort of thinking, 'Oh, I'd love to be with him', sort of thing.
I'm not getting those feelings at all. Now whether that's because of
the trauma I've been through – my libido's not quite as high as it
was – I don't know. But I am encouraged, let's put it that way. But
it would be wrong of me to say I've cracked it.

It is still fairly hard for me to think that I went through over 20
years of having sexual relationships with these youngsters and doing
the damage which I've done; not only to them but to my family, their
families and their friends, when the one thing that I wouldn't have
done consciously, was to hurt anyone. I am the biggest pacifist you
would ever wish to meet in your life. I wouldn't hurt a fly. And to
think now, that I have hurt what accumulatively must be hundreds
of people, is just too much. I can't forgive myself. I don't know how I
shall live with myself.

As I say, the sexual side of my relationships with these lads has
been something borne out of a long friendship, getting very, very
close and to me it seemed a natural progression. Sex to me has
been, always has been, just an expression of deep feeling – one for
another; and so it was with the lads. I would do the same to a
50-year-old as I would have done then to a 15-year-old.

That lad I was telling you about – several years ago, when this lot
hit the fan, I said to him, 'Thanks', I said, because, you know, 'I'm
much older than you', I said, 'How the heck do you think that having
sex with you, us two going to bed. How come you told them?' He
said, 'Kim, I've always looked at you as 15 years old, going on 50.'
And that, I think, is about the most accurate description anybody has
ever made of me – 15, going on 50. It was that sort of scenario;
interesting to know now that that's what he thought of me. It would
be interesting to talk to him now, not that I would make that effort. I
wouldn't put him in that position, but I would like someone to talk
to him, just to find out exactly what his views are now, I would be
most interested to hear. I think it would help put into context the
foul things that I've done and to reaffirm what they're saying. I might
be wrong, but I'm still having great difficulty in believing that I have

done so much damage, mentally, to these children – well, they are now adults. This is probably because I can't face having hurt people. I was hoping I might have sorted it out.

And it sort of drifted on from there; I've always felt that I had, you know, I wanted to help others and that's been, and still is, my sort of major concern in life. You know, through this therapy, they've called me selfish, because I was pursuing my own reasons for doing what I was doing, which rather made me stop and really have a look at myself. I didn't feel it that way at all. The help I was giving these victims was actual. It wasn't conjured up.

For instance, one of these lads had a mother who was a drug-taker. He had two younger sisters and was virtually their father. He had to look after his two baby sisters and his mother used to beat the hell out of him. His father used to go off down the club, drinking just to get out of the whole thing and didn't used to take any action with him. He was beaten up by his mum one day. He ran off and phoned me. And he told me what had happened and with that I phoned up the police and the Social Services and I left home and came down to see him. It was that sort of commitment I had with these lads, so what I was doing wasn't, in my eyes, just a vehicle to have a sexual relationship.

HARRY

The easy target features in Harry's account but this time within the context of a love at first sight meeting and a rescue. The child is portrayed as a victim of other children who is saved by the perpetrator, who is transformed into rescuer.

I think I'd been going up there for at least eight or nine months and suddenly one evening, we'd already got the children, the nor-mal group and they were there and they were having a soft drink and some crisps, which we usually started the session with. And suddenly this other boy appeared – he was ten. One of the social workers had brought him direct from his home instead of us pick-ing up because it was his first time. And I mean the only way that I could have described it is, I mean I took one look at him and I thought, 'Well, you know, this is it.' And the way he sort of smiled, you know, he had a – an incredible personality.

Now I know having done the core programme, this is all sort of excuses and all the rest of it, but I mean to me at that moment, I just took one look at him and I thought, 'Well', you know. 'He's just wonderful.' And his personality was such. He was so outgoing and right from the very start he sat down next to me and started talking to me and was so very, very friendly, and so easy to get on with. And so of course we went out on normal sessions. And I mean, he just sort of hung on to me all the time. I suppose he was lonely, I don't know. I think his situation was that he was very, very bright and he just despised other children. He couldn't get on with other children and he much preferred the company of adults – so that explains why he attached himself to me. But I was telling myself that, 'Oh, he attached himself to me because he likes me, he wants me.' And so I gave myself the permissions, you know, to go further with him than I did with the others; obviously, it started the same way.

VERNON

It is interesting to see how this former teacher obscures the abusive relationship with the problems of being a homosexual in a homophobic society. Throughout the account, he portrays himself as someone trying to ward off the attentions of a 'street-wise' boy from whom he can accept the reassurance that no harm was done.

The offence was having sex with an under-age boy. The point is, I'm a homosexual, always have been; I knew this before I was eight or nine years old. Whether I was born that way – something to do with my childhood, I have no idea, but I knew then. But of course in those days it was unmentionable, the word 'gay' hadn't even been invented and of course it was totally illegal. And so I had to face the fact that I was going to go through all my life without having any sexual relationships whatsoever. And I accepted that, but as time went on I found I was getting more and more frustrated; I had to find some sort of sexual outlet. It was just no good, I just couldn't keep it going. This came to a head when I came back to Britain to work at —— and that was just at the time when the law was changed.

It was too late, as far as I was concerned, because I was then 40 years old and over the top I reckoned – couldn't imagine anybody being interested in me. And then when we went comprehensive, purely by chance, without planning it or intending it, I met this young lad who, well, I got interested in him. I don't think frankly there was anything sexual to start with – that came later – but I gradually got more and more involved with this kid and he actually wanted to have sex with me – I didn't in fact suggest it to him – that's what mattered.

The thing that worried me was that he was getting far too dependent on me. He was expecting me to do everything, I think, and I decided, 'Okay, you're 14 years old, it's time you started to stand on your own feet, like I did.' But the trouble was, he was very vulnerable and I didn't want to upset him in any way. So I decided that my policy would be not to invite him to my house, not to suggest anything, but to leave it to him and if he wanted any help, he could come to me and I would give it to him. And I tried to make that clear to him, not by telling him, but from my manner, you see, and as a result the number of visits he made gradually dropped off, until it was – you know, only two or three times a year and I thought, you know, 'This is fine, this is excellent.' But then when he was 16, of course, he left school and I thought, 'Well that's it', you know, 'I won't see him again.' And I didn't see him for some time. And I got this pathetic letter from him saying, 'Oh, I do miss you. Why don't you ever write to me? I can't stay away.' So I went round. I picked him up and we came back to my house and we had sex again. And this went on intermittently and then he decided to journey on. And I thought, 'Well this really is it.'

And then I got a letter from him saying, 'Please come, it would be lovely to see you.' And I couldn't. I was already prepared; I had to go to school; I couldn't take a day off. So I wrote back a polite letter, saying, 'Look, I can't, really can't do this.' And then later on I met his father. The father said to me, 'He was terribly upset that you didn't go. He was really hurt about that.' So I thought, 'Oh well, perhaps it's best forgotten.' So I didn't bother to write to him and he didn't write to me for about a year and then I got another letter from him saying, 'I am very lonely, please let me come and stay with you. Could I come and live with you?' So I wrote back and said, 'No, you can't come and live with me, but if you want to come and visit then that's fine.'

And this fellow was really hurt about this and he came to me and he said, 'This is all your fault.' And I said, 'Look', I said, 'That's not fair. It's not entirely my fault. We did it together.' And I said, 'In any case, I wouldn't hurt anyone.' Anyway, shortly after that he got married and I didn't see him again. And I assumed that the reason was that he didn't want to tell his wife anything about us, so I didn't bother about it at all until about three years ago – no two years ago; it was only a few months before I came here in fact. One evening – winter's evening – there was a knock at my door and this chap was standing outside. I didn't recognise him at first and I said, 'Oh,' you know, 'You!' I said, 'Come in.' So he came in and we spent about an hour talking and had a coffee together. And he was talking about the old days, you know, and he said, 'I don't know what would have happened to me if you hadn't come into my life', and I said, 'Well, I'm pleased to see how well you've turned out.'

He's got five kids now. He's a very responsible family man, happily married. He's had a bit of bad luck with his jobs – but I mean, apart from that, he's done well. Yeah. And he said to me, 'That was very dangerous', he said, 'You having sex with me'. And I said, 'Yes, I suppose in retrospect it was, but I didn't think about it at the time.' And I said, 'Did it do any harm?' and he said, 'No, not at all', and I said, 'Well, that's the main thing. It didn't do any harm at all.' That was the last time I saw him.

It all seems terribly ironic to me, looking back now. I was naive. I mean, I'm not putting the blame on him, it was my fault more than his, because I was the adult; he was the child – albeit a very street-wise sort of child. I feel that if my circumstances had been different, the situation would never have cropped up, but I mean that's what life is like, isn't it?

The following two extracts show, first, the use of pornography to turn the innocence of childhood into adulthood, and second, the difficulty of extricating feelings of love and care from the realisation of the damage caused. The effect of being challenged is clearly evidenced by the oscillation between acceptance of, and scepticism about, the messages from other people. The honesty of the self-analysis contained in the second extract is suggested by the question of whether the subject would have abused his own children if he had been a father.

DAFYDD

I had a film; it wasn't even mine; there was no excuse there. One of the kids on the Wednesday afternoon – there was a school, bank, week's holiday, half-term, whatever they called it, leading up to Easter – he said, 'What's that film?' he said, 'That film on the front seat of your car.' And I thought, 'Sod it.' I put it on. I showed one girl and three or four boys, 12- or 13-year-olds. I put it on, left them in the room and about two minutes later, I thought,

'Sod it. What have I done?' I walked back in and switched it off. Said, 'Keep your mouths shut.' And I got 18 months, you know. I got 18 months suspended, for that.

RONNIE

I got in a relationship with a 15-year-old, who was a member of the family. I use the word 'relationship', but I've only ever had – with anybody – it's always been no more than just masturbation. I say no more, I know that's wrong, but I'm putting it into that context at this moment. That's not minimising it, because I know I've been minimising a lot over the years. This is something I've thought about since I've been here, the fact that I have minimised. I've minimised to such an extent that I've taken these things as acceptable and I've only been able to think clearly and step to one side since I've been arrested. It's very strange, I'm a person who's educated, so I should know better. That side of you says, 'You should know better.' And yet I've minimised the offence. I can use that word now. I would never use the word 'offence' for a long, long time. I've minimised it in my mind. I put it right.

The boys involved were usually between 13 and 16. I've been pondering tremendously since it's all come to light and I've had time to think. One – have I really harmed those people? All the experts tell me that I have. It's a terrible thing to say that, even now, that's why this core programme's come to be very good for me. At this moment now, I find it hard to accept, put it like that. I'm not saying that I don't believe it, that it's nonsense, but I find it hard to accept that I harmed those people.

We remained friends when the relationships stopped, you know, for a long time afterwards. There's one in particular, who lasted a long time. And time passed. Eventually I taught him to drive. He left school. He had a job. I knew the family very well, and I felt that he was a close, true friend. And we had a relationship until he was 17 and it continued afterwards, right up until last December, continued as friends, not as sexual friends. I don't know, this is something I do worry terribly about; have I hurt these pupils? I'm hoping to God I haven't. And yet all the indications are, from what I'm told and have been told, that I have. Possibly, when I go through the core programme, I will really find exactly how much I have hurt them.

To say I never intended to sounds bland, you know. You have your criminal in every prison who will say, 'I didn't mean to do it',

or something. I have to decide. I have to come to terms with it –
that it was nothing more than just pure lust on my part. What
was I getting out of it? Comfort definitely, I know that. Did I like
these people? Yes, I really did like them. I would have done anything for these people. And yet, I liked them so much, was I now
hurting them? And that hurts, you know. The people, I really liked
them in every way and now I'm beginning to think I've hurt the
people I like most. And that's hard to think.

Don't forget now, these were all ex-pupils. These were ex-pupils,
so they'd been through the school, they'd been through my, my
class, my teaching. And I suppose basically, simply because children of the age I was teaching don't – to get back to what we said
earlier on, if they were giving the lead in a sense, giving me
something to pick up on, that's the way to put it – of course
children that age don't give you those things to pick up on in the
same way; though in one case, the person I had the longest – I use
this word relationship now, because I don't know another word for
it – the longest period of time with, actually, that started – he was
the youngest one who I did abuse – before he was 12. From the
point of view of caring, honestly, I cared for them all. There's no
doubt about that.

Yes, I saw them as relationships. I saw them in that way. The
probation officer I talked with said that's one term that can't ever
be accepted. That may be right. But I did ... This person ... We
were friends. He's been through heterosexual relationships – girlfriends, etc. – and I can't see in that sense that it's harmed him,
and yet it might have done. You see, for all I know, it may have
hurt him. I need to ask him. And if I have hurt him, it hurts
terribly, because it really ... He really did mean a tremendous lot to
me. I cared for him really out of this world. I really did care for
him. If there's such a thing as being in love, I suppose that was it.
In that case he was a tremendous help to me.

This sexual side of the relationship was just something that had
happened and it didn't matter it was over. The relationship started
again two or three months later. He wanted it to start. He took all
the lead. I followed. And this relationship continued with big gaps
until he was older and he went through a very bad time. And it
stopped at that period and we never restarted again, even though
we remained friends.

I think that, in my case, the fact that I found it so difficult to
make relationships with adults – it's the only relevant word you
could use – adult males, and how easy it was to make a relationship with non-adult males. And I think it's probably, as well,

something else I'm obviously guilty of. My ego was definitely given a boost that these people wanted my company, wanted to tell me their private lives, wanted to confide in me, wanted to lean on me. I obviously got, I did, I know this, I had a tremendous comfort out of that. If only I hadn't gone the full way in sexual abuse. I'm sure perhaps I could have had that comfort, which in a way we all do need.

I suppose – that's the very phrase – I wanted to be a father, and yet if I was a father, I'd have been a bad father. I don't know. If I'd been a father, would I have abused my own children? I don't know. That's something I'll never be able to answer. I actually do remember as a 24-year-old suddenly realising that I wouldn't be a father, that I would not be a husband and a father and I cried my eyes out, like a five-year-old. It finally dawned on me that this is it, this is never going to be you. And in time you get used to something. You don't live with that kind of atmosphere, you accept that. But I suppose I crept into abuse through that need, and I just didn't control it. Other things came in as well. I still, part of me still feels today, definitely, that I'm not quite all there in a sense. That's a sad, stupid thing. I still feel today, possibly, that there is something wrong with me, possibly, but the psychiatrist wouldn't actually say that you had got something definitely wrong with you; that you are suffering from some delusion, or something or other. And maybe a part of me would like him to say that. That would give me an excuse again, wouldn't it? I suppose nobody ever keeps excuses as well as you I don't know the answer. Because I repeat myself – is it just that I've been a fool? Is it just that I'm useless? I don't know what the answer is.

DAVID

Through the language of the treatment programme David elucidates a detailed and graphic representation of Finkelhor's (1984) theoretical model of child sexual abuse.

And also by subduing. Using your mind to subdue any sense of harm that it can cause, 'I won't do any harm. It will be all right. I won't be caught.' All those things come into mind. I think I created a doubt. I created a consensual lie to myself and to my victims. I don't think my victims would – did even – when evidence was taken from them, there was a certain degree ... I'd convinced them that they were 'partakers of', not 'being done to'. So I convinced them and myself, which frightens me even more and appals me even more. My behaviour was that I'd fooled myself into being an abuser ..., that almost, I'd coped with it. I'd coped, therefore they'll cope. Therefore – onward from there.

It sounds hard and callous and is again something which reminds me of what I hated with my – in my family group. Cold, callous, 'I'll take what I want', attitude, which was denying the person I know myself to be, as caring, loving, tender by contrast. I almost dropped myself and took up what they wanted me to be, 'If you want it, get it.' And I'll use a whole mixture of things there. Yeah, I do. I find it very frightening that I was so ... I find it frightening that I was so stupid and so conscious without conscience. I know what I did. I knew what I did was wrong. I know what I did was wrong, but I still did it. That's what makes me frightened. But I chose to disabuse the concept of victim and replace it with the concept of consensual – consensual acts, whatever you want to call it. And the fact that there was never any physical force, or violence, I did have a consensual lie. But now you identify the fact that there is no need for violence, because you 'groom' people, you prepare people, you normalise things. And people then accept the normalisations you have created within the relationship between two people.

I can see where I am and where I've been, but then I chose to switch it off. And there I would see. I share each contribution from my past of the ability to switch off one world and switch on another world. I could move freely between these different worlds and survive them all, as I had to survive. I moved from one to the other when I wanted to. But obviously because of the situation that I was in, it created an opportunity for me to use ... They would trust 'grooming' opportunities on all occasions. And again, it's ... it's something which I feel a huge sense of guilt about now; that I have done that; which perhaps I didn't feel at the beginning, because the – I think – I feel – it's all in feel – feelings. This is self-pity. I've lost everything I've done, you know. Now I realise that I've thrown it away. I'm losing ... And that I've not only betrayed myself, I feel I have, I feel other people here have betrayed themselves, like I betrayed myself. I betrayed others, but I also feel that I have another dimension where I betrayed my priesthood, which is perhaps even more important to me than myself. So I'm feeling a huge sense of shame and guilt in that dimension as well. And so that's again a point. That's two, two dimensions in my life, again, which I don't like, which I carry, rightly carry; guilt and shame for myself and guilt and shame for my office, my work.

But when I actually sit down and rationalise things, I realise it's the same guilt and shame, because it's me. But I have that tendency to keep it on then. I feel so bad because I'm carrying two sides, you see, it's almost a community guilt and a personal guilt and it's centred on the one person.

Yes, why shouldn't I? It's my fault and I feel it's very much my ... There's nobody else to fault or blame; it's my responsibility entirely. And I've – stupid side of it is that I've ... so stupid, stupid – I've recognised that from the very beginning anyway. But I've had to cloak it with the lying to myself, otherwise I wouldn't have done it and I realise that now. And I realise that is also a key to future not offending – the fact that I've accepted responsibility and I realise and accept the lie that I placed to block out these ideas and knowledge of guilt and responsibility and that, that is illegal. And I think that as long as I maintain that knowledge, then I can't reoffend, because I don't want to reoffend. You know, it's a stupid phrase, 'Oh well I'll never reoffend'. I think the only thing you can put in there is, 'I don't *want* to reoffend', because I've seen it through myself, through my own life.

Yeah. I look back now and I wish I hadn't done it, first of all. And I wish I'd maintained the strong friendship in a proper relationship that I had, which I took ... which I built my abuse on. I wish that I'd done that, and been able now to see the development of those people to adults and on from there. I feel now the abuse was entirely selfish, whereas then I saw it very much as consensual. 'They wouldn't be here if they didn't want to do this.' They were between 14 and 19. That they were old – I felt then, they were old enough and street-wise enough to not be there. But now I see that what I did was that I conditioned them. I normalised my abuse so they didn't really have any choice. They were just drawn in by the ... I feel a complete bastard about it, which I really feel about myself. And I've destroyed not only their lives, families, friends – just goes out in a spread – 'cos I'm concerned, for their ... and my own family and friends. And there's a huge sense of betrayal as well. I feel that I wish I could put it all back in order, but alas ... put it all right; then I could go on as normal. But I wish that through some way or other, you could put it all right and just go on knowing that they'd be all right. And the great concern I have, within myself, is that I hope they're going to be all right for the future.

Targeting

KIM

The importance of power – in this instance as a result of the expertise and charisma of the abuser set against the paucity of the life experience of the potential victims – and the manipulation of other unwitting allies, are both underlined in Kim's account.

I was asked to go and visit a special school many, many years ago, as part of my job. At that time I was interested in climbing and I was an instructor. And the headmaster and me got on to the subject of climbing, naturally, as climbing to me wasn't a sport, it was a disease which I'd caught. He said, 'Would you help me?' And I said, 'Yes'. Now, looking at this – it's interesting – this pathetic distortion. Now I went in there to do this, but I was set up ... So I went. I became the most popular thing since sliced bread in that school, and the kids and I got on like a house on fire. But these were all kids from the back end of ——. They'd got no bloody hopes, they'd never done anything like this before. So I was taking them – once they'd learnt how to climb and all sorts of things – exciting places and I was giving them a right shot in the arm.

The headmaster saw how I was getting on with these boys and he pulled me aside one day and he said, 'We've got a problem child', he said, 'that's not a boarder. He comes in daily,' he said. 'And he wants a sort of father-figure, to sort of keep an eye on him – take him out occasionally, and just generally sort of be his friend. Can you do this?' And I said, 'Yes'. And this guy's name was ——, ten years old then. And he and I became firm friends and he was one of my victims, you know, eventually. But that took three years to develop into a sexual relationship and he was one of the guys who has stood with me right the way through it – at court. And out of that school, I suppose, I had two or three more victims over the course of a few years. But these were guys that got close to me and I got close to them. I suppose you could say that every kid in that school was a vulnerable target. Why I chose – they chose me or I chose them – I don't know. I can't describe that – really just characters that got on well with each other and that was the way it went. And a lot of my victims were attracted to me – or I attracted them – I don't know how you want to look at it. With the climbing, it was sport and activities.

HARRY

Harry, in his description of the premeditation underpinning his offending, gives a clear illustration of the implementation of a strategy – ironically involving the use of skills learned from playing games – against vulnerable victims. The account is also vivid in its elucidation of an offence cycle.

I can recognise that rather more now, having done the core programme, but I mean, at the time I didn't sort of think it through quite in those terms. Looking back on it, I see now that it was all very much in my mind, you know, if I do this I might well meet someone who, you know, will take a fancy to me and whatever. So that was certainly in my mind, although I probably wasn't aware of it, certainly not to the extent that I'm aware of it now, you know, looking back on it.

I suppose it started when I was in ——. I don't really think the thought came to me very much before then, although obviously I would see youngsters around who I would find attractive and sort of perhaps think about them, but I certainly didn't do anything about it. But when I left —— and went to live with —— – when things started to get a bit rocky, when I felt he was moving away – I was sort of casting my eyes elsewhere.

At about that time, there was an advertisement in the ... I think it was a newspaper, one of the local newspapers – it might have been in a shop window, I'm not sure. Partly because I was interested in games, that sort of thing, I thought, 'Oh, you know, that will be an area where I might find someone who'd be interested in playing games.' And I thought, 'Well, that would be a soother and also I might get to know some youngsters who I might develop some sort of friendship with.' And so I did that. I went along to them and offered my services as it were, saying, telling them, what my interest was. And they were very keen and they said, 'Oh yes', you know. 'I'm sure the children will find that very interesting.' And so I did that. I went along once a month and I took a selection of games.

Now, as it happened, the child that was most interested in the games was actually a girl. And she was very interested and she wanted to come back to my house and, you know, play these games and all this sort of thing and of course the parents said, 'No'. But she had a younger brother and he was not as interested as her, but was quite interested and they'd allow him. And I remember thinking at

the time how stupid it was, because, you know, I found the girl very
nice and I liked her very much and obviously we had the same
interest, but I wasn't the least bit interested in her in a sexual way;
whereas the younger brother who's about 11, I thought, 'Well', you
know, 'he's very sweet'. And, you know, 'He's a bit young, but he's
very attractive.' And so he came back to my house with the sister on
the first occasion and then he came on his own a couple of times. All
that happened is we played games, and it was nice to have his
company. I did sort of fantasise about what might have happened
afterwards, but that was as far as it went.

But then I suppose, thinking back, I was thinking to myself,
'Well, this ... I'm not really getting anywhere with this. I mean,
it's nice to have the company of these young people, but I'm not
actually achieving anything. I'm not getting anything out of it
myself, really.' And there was a ... I think it was a sort of
voluntary organisation in —— who were coordinating people who
were prepared to do voluntary work. So I went to see them and
stipulated work with children, and they said, 'Oh, well, would
you mind working with mentally retarded children?' And I said,
'No, I wouldn't mind doing that'. And they said, 'Well, we'll
send you out to see someone at the hospital.'

So I went out to the hospital, and at first they tend to sort of
show you what they call the difficult cases, you know, they try to
put you off. They show you into a ward where there are all those
sort of people as much as to say, 'Well', you know, 'if you can't
handle this, then we don't want you', sort of thing.

Well, I'd obviously gone there with, at the back of my mind,
you know, sort of fairly normal children. So it was a bit of a sort
of shock to me, but I thought well, you know, they are human
beings and I was helping feeding them, you see. And although they
were physically not at all attractive, I felt a very strong sort of
mental attraction to them, because they seemed to have a personality, which was rather hidden inside this sort of shell, which
looked rather grotesque. And of course, some of them that I would
... most of them that I was helping to feed, certainly were, although they were physically sort of 16, 17, they were like babies.
And so I found a bit to my surprise that I actually quite enjoyed
sort of being there and being with them. And gradually they got
me to do more things which involved the wider circle of children
there.

And then it was some years – no not years – well, a couple of
years, couple of years later, after I'd left ... 'cos I had this holiday
and I left —— and I got this job working for ——. And again I

started to think, you know, feeling a bit lonely, I'll try and you know, sort of do some voluntary work in the area. And I worked with the local cubs.

Now actually, I would have preferred to work with the scouts, but they didn't have a vacancy in the scouts, so they said, 'Oh, would you help out with the cubs?' and so I went as an assistant. Now it didn't come to pass that I took over as leader there, but I did of another troop. But some of the lads that ... the older ones, the older cubs who were just about leaving for scouts, I got to know them and I continued to know them after they went into the scouts. And they used to come over to the cubs that I was looking after and they would be assistants to me, you see. They were only – there were two of them basically.

VERNON

The rescuing theme re-emerges in this story. The future abuser firstly rescues the young boy from bullying, then from an uncaring headmaster and finally from squalid home conditions. Almost Pygmalion in its tone, the relationship is presented as one of nurturing and education, without any reference to other motivations.

The perchance factor was that it was the beginning of the September term – it was just a week into the school, and morning break. I went up to my room to prepare for a sixth form lesson coming up. And a young woman who taught in the room opposite came rushing in and she said, 'There's a boy downstairs in the toilets, crying.' So I rushed down to the boys' toilets and there was this little 11-year-old lad, and there was a crowd of kids just watching him. And I took him upstairs to get him away from the other kids.

I put him in my other little office up there. He was in quite a state. He was sort of crying and he was actually filthy; he was covered in mud; his clothes were like rags, as though he'd never had a wash; he stank. I didn't know who he was at all. Anyway, I calmed him down a bit and then I took him downstairs to the headmaster. And I said to him, 'I think we'd better do something about this kid.' And to my astonishment, the Head just didn't want to know, or he couldn't care less and he sent this kid off. He said, 'Get back to your lessons' and he said to me, 'Don't waste my time.'

I was absolutely shattered as I thought this kid was being bullied. I thought, 'Well, maybe, maybe it wasn't serious. But, I mean, something's got to be done about this kid.' So I made a point of getting to know him. I'm not sure if it was that day or the day after, or whatever, but I got hold of him and I persuaded him to let me take him home. He'd never been in a car in his life, so he was thrilled.

I took him to his home and it was the most horrendous one I'd ever seen. He lived with his mother and there was virtually no furniture in the house at all. The walls were sort of black with soot and the place was actually filthy, you see. So I thought, 'Well, no, I'd better do something about this.' So I got to know this kid. I got the mother's permission for him to come to my house and I gave him a bath and I bought him some clothes and gave him a meal and by talking to him I discovered that he was virtually illiterate. So I helped him learn to read and write.

He couldn't tell the time. I had an old wrist-watch, so I showed it to him and I said, 'Would you like it?' So he said, 'Yeah' and I said, 'Well, you're not having it', I said, 'not until you can tell the time'. And he used to come to me every morning break at school and I had this wrist-watch and set a time and said, 'What time is it?' And when he could tell the time, I gave it to him. I gradually got more and more involved with him. He was a thoroughly nice kid and the extraordinary thing about him was, he was so well spoken. He never swore, never said anything that was impolite. I just couldn't understand how a kid like that could live in that situation.

DAFYDD

The early stages of the relationship described in the following extract are characterised by the existing status of the child as a victim of somebody else and Dafydd's identification with her vulnerability. The trigger for the subsequent offending appears to be a build-up of stress and problems in his own life. Interestingly, the extract begins with the victim's vulnerability and ends with that of the offender.

And my victim – she was 14 at the time – she told my colleague, female colleague, that her uncle had been very seriously raping her since she was about 11 years old. And she didn't want to tell the police because she had the reputation of being a liar. And I was called in and my colleague said, 'Would you mind telling Dafydd, or do you want me to tell him what you've just told me?'

She broke down and cried, but she got it out. And this was the start of my downfall. I actually said to her 'Look, wouldn't it be better if you told a policewoman, or a policeman? Lots of police in the community are really good friends of ours now. They don't come to arrest the kids any more, they come to play football with them and play darts and pool with them.' 'No, no, no, mustn't tell the police, no, no, no. My dad would kill me, oh no.'

The girl had lots of problems within the club. She had ... I can understand ... she ... because she didn't have any friends and certainly her mum and dad didn't get on, or she didn't get on with her mum and dad, she was always pushed to the side; nobody wanted to befriend her ... trying to be the centre of attraction, so that everybody likes her; need to be liked. And I really felt for her, maybe with my own background, my own upbringing, I saw this in her.

RONNIE

Below, the ambiguities involved in self-analysis are represented in a fascinating reflection on why the abuse took place. On the one hand, Ronnie acknowledges the issue of his victims' vulnerability, expressed in their need for a father-figure, but on the other, apportions responsibility to them for their sexual remarks. His interpretation of those remarks is seen as irrelevant.

When I say that I kept in touch with them; they kept in touch with me, in the sense that, the background to the school, it was an open affair, in the sense these people went to secondary schools – boys and girls – and they knew that the school was always there for them to come back to; use the photocopier, etc. And of course there were computers that they were allowed to use as well. So that was how they would come back, but both sexes. And I didn't ever, not in one single case, did I go out of my way and say, 'I'm picking him.' None of them worked like that.

I've been thinking a lot. How did these relationships ...? And I know now you must ... the relationships, because you can't have a relationship with somebody under a certain age. So I haven't got a better word to use at the moment. I've also been looking in my mind to see if there was a pattern. I've been asking, you see, is there a pattern in these people? Are they ...? Were they all somehow vulnerable, in the sense that they were turning to me as another kind of father-figure? And I was letting them down? I've let them down. To an extent I feel there is that. A pattern in the sense that ...? I can't say that one or two of them were from bad homes. No, there are many ways of registering homes, financially, emotionally and so on. I think some of them were looking for a father-figure, or a leader of some sort and they chose me and I let them down. That hurts now, when I'm thinking more about it. I don't know if this is right.

Not consciously. I can say, I'm frightened of saying this. I feel frightened of saying this because people will say, 'There we are, he's finding a way out.' In so many, most, all of the people I was involved with, I wasn't the one that introduced sexual matters. Possibly, once they introduced something in a broad way, I picked on it. They made sexual remarks. Somehow, whereas I should have shut it out, I didn't do it. So I was – in that sense – I was picking up something which I should have stopped. I didn't ever go to one ... I didn't think, 'Right, I'm going to make this number "x" a victim.' I never thought of them as victims. I know that's not an excuse, but I obviously had a different way of homing in, if that's the right word. Obviously, I was homing in, I must have been. Doesn't make it any better, but I didn't go out scouring for people, looking for people. And yet they were available. And I abused them – simple as that. I abused them. And I'm regretting it, not because I'm here – being here's no problem – but I think ... I was talking in this very room actually, with the chaplain. I had a long chat with him when I came in here. Possibly I was in ... I'd even been looking, looking for punishment. I suppose looking for punishment means that you want things put right.

JAMES

In the next extract, deliberate and clearly thought out manipulation of the work environment and everybody in it, is placed alongside the day-to-day business of caring for children. The occupational role and the abusive role are never more markedly pronounced.

I mean I don't think I've got a very high sex drive – sex has never been incredibly important to me – but obviously I'm a normal human being, I get urges. My sex life was now pretty well non-existent and I started looking at the children as perhaps a substitute, well not perhaps, as a substitute. I think even at the time, deep down, I realised what I was doing, because while I was working at the school I didn't let anything happen. I would be around the children a lot, while they were showering and things like that and perhaps that was enough for me at that time.

I had been in —— for quite a while and I thought, 'Well done, I'm living here. This is the area I want to live, find a job around here.' And I got a temporary job at a school club and again, inappropriate behaviour, but no actual criminal behaviour there. I was only on a term to term contract there, because they said, you know, 'We have a full quota of child care officers.' What I was doing, I was helping out in place of an actual assistant. And they said, 'You know, we might have a vacancy in about six months, we might not.'

Dead easy. I mean, I can admit now, I was manipulating the system. There are one or two ways of manipulating the system – very easy. I manipulated the staff to the extent that, you know, doing every sleep-in – Monday, Tuesday, Wednesday, Thursday, right, because I was in the senior year now. The staff thought nothing of seeing me around the school at night. Whereas, of course, if you're not on sleep-in, people would think, 'What the hell's he doing?' But with me they thought, 'Oh, he's on sleep-in, it's all right.'

A lot of the staff there were women; it's their second job and they treat it as a very happy holiday. Come twenty-to-ten, it's getting to knocking-off time at night. There's a mad rush for the staff room to get all the coats so you're out of there by ten o'clock. And I used that. 'Don't worry, I'll sort that for you. I'm on sleep-in anyway, so it doesn't matter. Go on, you go home, because your husband will be expecting you and I'll deal with this.' So I was using that as well; I was manipulating everybody really, the school rules, the staff and obviously the victims.

Yes, that's quite true. Yes, I am very good at building up that sort of rapport with children. I remember we had a classic example at the school. This young lad – must have been about ten when he came in to the school – he was brought up by the police and the Social Services. So I sat there for three hours with this child and he just talked, and gradually I get the response back, you know and obviously from then on, I could do no wrong, you know, in the child's eyes. And I really got that child to sort of come out of his shell, because for three hours I sat with him and that's the sort of rapport I had. Now whether some of that was targeting him as an eventual victim ... But some of that is doing my job, or what I saw as my job – trying to help children, because I do care.

That's the problem. That is the crux of the question. I would always try and be fair, pick my time. Even those, if I can put it so crudely, I didn't fancy. I wouldn't say, 'No, go away, I don't want to know you.' I would still try and do my best to involve them.

But then of course, you put the extra-special effort into your targets by evening runs. I think the holidays were the weakness for that, the school holidays as well.

I had become very close with one of the kids. The parents used to come round and say, 'Oh, he's being a little sod, will you come down and sort him out?' So I was getting, I was manipulating the parents. I was worming my way in, you know, 'Ask James if he knows this. Ask James. Yeah, we can let —— go off with James, because James is a good bloke,' you know. 'Innit nice of James to take him to a football match?' Again, where the Residential Worker – sorry – where the abuser had stopped and the Residential Worker took over ... I mean 90 per cent of that was abuser and 10 per cent of that was Residential Worker. You're trying to do your job, trying to help the kids sometimes, but, yes, 90 per cent of that, in those situations was getting parents used to me having their children.

In one case ... there's one child we've got in the school, and he was a real bad boy and I thought, 'Now, wait a minute, if I can be seen to be able to handle you, to cope with you, and get you in my unit ... And once you're in my Unit, I'm in complete control of you.' So I deliberately set out to win the confidence of that child and – not exactly to control – but try and work on what it is with him to present more – behave more appropriately. So in that situation, yes I knew what I was doing to people round me. Perhaps I wouldn't admit it to myself. In fact, I wouldn't have admitted it to myself then. But yes, looking back now, I knew then what I was doing.

I hope I'm not talking out of turn, but the way the headmaster there deals with the kids is through fear – puts the fear of God into them. He has too much involvement in my view, whereas to me a headmaster should be some sort of periphery god that you are called to when you create your ultimate sin. But no, he was there all the time ... And he shouts and he bawls, and he stops television, and he stops this and he stops that. And that's when they're seven, eight, nine, ten. But by the time they're starting eleven, twelve, they're thinking, 'Bollocks, mate. I'm standing up to you.' And as soon as they stand up to him, 'Woof, senior school can have him. I can now no longer intimidate, threaten and get my way by my method, so whack! You can have him.' Dreadfully certain.

Look, in that way, it helped me by having my own union. I was the only one who worked the leavers' union. Because it was only open Monday to Friday, I actually spent every weekend going home.

And I think the headmaster found my views so diametrically opposed
to his views on child care ... When I first went there I was working
the normal shift, which is, you know, morning, then afternoon and
night off, morning off, afternoon on, evening shifts ... morning on,
like that and doing every other weekend. But because I was then
carrying on working for the little ones, he found it very ... our views
were so, you know, I didn't like the way things were going. You know
to me, they should be getting more treats on the weekends and things
like that. It shouldn't be like just any school anywhere.

But I think he thought, 'For god's sake, how can I get him out
of school for the weekend so I've got the little ones? He's good
with dealing with the old ones. He can keep the old ones out of
my hair. I know I'll give him the union, the leavers' union and
then he can work Monday, Tuesday, Wednesday, Thursday, Friday
up to dinner time. When they go home, he's got the weekend off.
Instead of having a day off during the week, he can have the
weekend; gets him out of my way. He's quite good at handling
that. Keeps the seniors out of my hair – ideal solution.' So it was
offered to me and I said, 'Yes, thanks.'

I mean it was set up in such a way. There is the union section,
and then there are several units which are the senior receptacle. Now
God help the seniors if they were in the junior section, unless they
were there for the nurse, because the sick room was in there. But
obviously the staff had to go in. So sometimes the kid – perhaps he's
been sent to bed or something – and the night duty supervisor who I
got on very well with, manipulated him round nicely to my way of
thinking, would say, 'Can you just nip up and see so-and-so ... Can
you just nip up and sort of make sure he's all right.'

I was the one – a lot of the kids saw me as the one – not exactly
who was on their side, but who they could come and talk to and I
would mediate for them with the headmaster and things like that.
They were all looking forward to the day when they could get in the
leavers' union, because then you have the little treats of cookie
nights, you know, you could stay up late at night, as long as you
abide by certain rules and this sort of thing. So the whole set-up
really was paradise for me, you know, it fell into my lap beautifully.

DAVID

*David indicates that his priesthood wasn't a route into his abusing
and then explains how all-enveloping the process of abusing became
in his life.*

I was a priest before I was an abuser. I wasn't an abuser who became a priest. I think that's the important element which I worked out within myself. I don't feel that I was an abuser who became a priest to abuse, working with youngsters or whatever and finding it as a means to an end. That was something which I thought of – I had to think that through, because it was something again, that I was afraid of. And having thought it through I felt then, I still feel now, that I was a priest a long time before I was an abuser. And the abuse became an element within my life, which was as a priest. The fact that I was working with people who I could take advantage of because of my trust and my position obviously made an easier situation than if I'd been a coal miner or a bus driver, or whatever.

But having read quite a lot around the subject now – you have social workers, teachers, etc, working alongside young people who find themselves in a similar situation to myself. I've got to be careful that I don't justify – oh, that's the wrong word. I can't think of the word. Because I was working with young people, I abused them. If I hadn't been working with young people, would I have gone out and looked for one to abuse? See what I mean? I'm frightened that I'm putting in there a little sort of excuse for myself and just saying, 'Oh well, it's only because they were there.'

Being alone was one of the huge factors, I think. If you're part of a social group, if you're part of a bunch of people, you don't have time to brood, to create opportunities for abuse, because you've got to create a whole world. Your whole world's got to be created around your abusing, to cover it up, just to have the time within you, your life, to abuse. I know it sounds very clinical, but I think if you've got a bunch of friends and you're involved socially with people more, then I'm sure it avoids it. You don't have the opportunities to relate to people who you shouldn't be relating to. Because to relate to somebody who you're going to offend against, you have to lower your age and raise theirs. Your desire to do that takes an awful lot of effort and pretence. And so I think being alone gives you that time to do it. I'm sure it's a contributory factor.

Grooming

KIM

Kim believes that the fact that the abuse was part of a relationship which was based on love and affection makes it moral. In his view, he provided something essential that was missing from the lives of his victims and, interestingly, what also appears to have been missing from his childhood.

Consequently with these relationships later on in my life, I could see ... I had no guilt at all about them. I knew what I was doing was illegal, but I couldn't see that it was immoral, because what I was doing was giving love and affection, in every sense of the word. It wasn't just a physical thing, it was a feeling, a total relationship, with a huge commitment on my side, to them, to their needs. If I saw that they were getting into trouble in any way, I would be quite stern with them and you know, I would discipline them as well, not physically, no, no physical discipline, but by my actions I would, you know. I used to take them out and give them treats occasionally, and if they'd done something wrong I wouldn't do that. They'd know they'd done this and the trip would be off for the next ... whenever it was, which used to cut them pretty hard, because those trips were quite important to them, because most of their homes were ... There was none of that sort of thing around in their homes. There was no love, or compassion, or treats. Some of them lived in complete squalor. And I suppose there are two sides of looking at that. You know, because they were living like that, they were easy victims; and the other way that I was looking at it, because they were living like that, I was giving them something that they wouldn't otherwise have had. And I felt that I didn't have that sort of love and tenderness given to me when I was a kid and I would have loved it so much and I gave it to these kids.

HARRY

The careful planning and very gradual, almost imperceptible, process of drawing the victim in, coupled to awareness of the levels of protection available from key adults are very clearly described by Harry.

I met two boys in particular who were mentally retarded. They were both very affectionate and I would, you know, be working in the ward and they would be doing various things, playing, watching television, going outside on the swings, things like that. And I got, you know, quite a lift from sort of being with them, because they were affectionate. I mean nothing of a sexual nature took place, of course, because, you know there were staff and other people around.

I mean, if I'd have had the opportunity I daresay I would have gone further, but it was just the fact that they would very readily come and sit on your lap and put their arm round you and kiss you and do things like that. I was doing that for several months and looking back on it now I suspect that one of the senior nurses thought that I was a bit too affectionate, particularly with these two. And rather than sort of go through official channels and do anything about it, because possibly they didn't have any evidence. I mean, if he'd have spoken to the boys, they would have either not have been able to convey much to him or, you know, because nothing very exceptional happened, I mean just touching their leg or something like that, there wouldn't have been a lot there anyway. So, I think what he decided to do, he came ... because he came to me and said, 'Oh, don't come next week Harry, because we've got a problem. There's a case of food poisoning. And so we're having no people from outside.' And so that was next week and then I phoned up the following week, 'Oh, no don't come, we've still got a problem.' And he was sort of putting me off and putting me off. And every time I phoned up it was ... there was some reason why he didn't want me to come. And eventually I sort of got the message that, you know, I wasn't really wanted there.

I invited —— to my home. At first his parents weren't at all keen – by that time he was about 12 and his parents weren't at all keen. And they said, 'It's all right for him to sort of go to —— and things like that, but not there.' Then eventually, he did come, but he came with his elder brother, and they stayed for the day. And he was inside the house with me and we were playing on the computer and various things and his brother was there some of the time, but some of the time he went out and had a walk. I showed him round the house and then he had a walk in the grounds. So —— and I were alone for a while and that happened a couple of times, and then he started coming on his own and I did begin to entertain thoughts that, you know, something might develop. But he then started bringing some friends, which I felt sort of two ways about.

Then one or two of the other children who used to sit on my lap in the minibus, including some girls, gradually got eased out and it was —— that was always sitting on my lap. And if another child was to sit on my lap, he'd pull them off. Well, of course I could have said, 'No, it's his turn, or her turn, or whatever', I could have said, 'No, —— you sit over there', but I didn't. And so

—— got so that he expected to sit on my lap every time, which he did. And again, I went through the very care ... cautious touching him on the leg, because I felt if I did any more, again I'd frighten him off. But I know it's ... they say it's an excuse, but I mean he just seemed more receptive than the others. He just seemed that he actually liked being touched and he liked being fondled and that's as far as it went in the mini-bus.

When he first came to visit me he was coming for the day on Saturday. And there were other children there and other adults occasionally and so we weren't on our own. And we'd perhaps be there and he'd be playing on the computer and there was another boy and he used to come round – he used to hang around the Close a lot. And again his mother would, you know, sort of say, 'Can you look after him for a while?' Now actually, I wasn't attracted to him and he ... in a way, he was a nuisance, because I wanted to be there with —— on his own, but I couldn't very well say no. So he used to come in and very often I had male adult friends there as well, because I'd had visits over the weekend. So it wasn't an ideal time, but what used to happen was that because —— wanted attention all the time, even though there were other people there, a certain amount of offending took place, because he would sit on my lap and I would stroke his leg and I would kiss him and things like that, even though there were other people there. And I mean, thinking back on it, I did some ridiculous things, you know, in front of other people, but it just sort of gradually evolved to that. I was doing more and more and more. And certainly if it was only the other child there – he was about 14 or 15, —— then was 11 – if he was there as opposed to an adult, I would actually kiss him and we'd perhaps be sat watching television and he'd cuddle up and kiss quite – quite passionately, you know, if the other lad was looking the other way, because he'd be watching television or sometimes he'd go into the kitchen. While he was in the kitchen or something like that we'd kiss, so it – it got quite a lot more intense, in spite of the fact that there were occasions with other people there. But then I said to him that it would be nice if it were just the two of us and he agreed to that and said, 'Yes, it would', and he asked his mother if he could come round.

So he asked his mother in the first place, you know, could he come down on Friday night and stay over the weekend. And I expected there to be a problem about that, but there wasn't. I mean, I daresay she had no suspicions. I mean after all, he'd been coming down to me for several months and was always pleading with her to be able to come down, so she wouldn't have seen any difficulties there. So she said, 'Yes, fine', you know, 'you can go

down on Friday.' I'd meet him off the bus to start with and then
eventually he'd make his own way down. But to start with, I'd go
to the bus and meet him. She put him on the bus and then I'd
pick him up off the bus. And then he'd stay and she'd come and
collect him on Sunday evening, about tea-time. And so, of course,
that meant that we were on our own Friday night all through the
night – on Saturday there would be other people there – and Saturday night and again Sunday morning and afternoon. And I got
emotionally involved with him. I mean, as I say, it wasn't sex, it
wasn't sex at that time. I was emotionally involved with him. I felt
responsible for him. And he used to come to my house about once
a month and he would stay the night. I had this spare bed. And I
used to take him to the cinema, or take him out for a picnic, or
take him to the zoo, something like that. You see, he never got
out anywhere.

DAFYDD

*The core programme has helped Dafydd to recognise the steps that
he took to manoeuvre himself into a situation where he could
abuse. His insight is considerable and he is able to see that it was
a very slow process.*

I don't use it as an excuse or a reason – the fact that the government rate-capped ... The only way we were going to survive was by
going co-ed – boys and girls. I don't use that as an excuse at all;
it's no reason. My downfall, really, was taking too much attention
and care of one specific young female. And allowing myself, even
steering myself, to getting into a position which was very, very
wrong.

Something I learnt on the core programme was the fact that
you must have thought this through, because you lost a hell of a
lot – you've thrown it all away; must have been a damn good
reason for you to have done that. And there are certain steps that
– whether it be deep in the recesses – but you must have gone
through those steps, different stages, to actually get to the position
where you offend. And yes, I got into a position of trust – my
victim trusted me very much. I gave myself all the permissions, I
allowed my fantasies to take me on to the next stage, which was
giving myself permission. It's not a fast process, it's one that is
very, very slow; crawling along.

Being in close proximity, it was easy. If there was ever a case where – and there were many – where kids were, other kids, were slagging —— off, I would be the one that would separate the two and rather than get the parties to talk about it, take —— to one side, 'There, there, there', you know, 'I'm your friend'.

Perpetration

KIM

Kim accepts that the age difference made the sex wrong, but he nevertheless openly describes his enjoyment of it.

The relationships that we developed were very caring relationships on both sides. The sexual side developed over a very long period of time – it wasn't instant by any means. It started off with, sort of, friendship and then, as we got closer, it was just a cuddle, a kiss and then it just sort of developed from there. It seemed at the time, a completely natural progression of feelings between two people. Of course, looking back at it now, the age difference was totally wrong. But this was how it was when I was a youngster; this was the same sort of relationship that I had with the lads around me then.

I'm a little bit confused as to where and why I took up with youngsters again, after I'd gained quite satisfactory adult relationships and I don't really know what brought that on. It certainly had ... not consciously, I never had any conscious thoughts on having sex with these youngsters when I first got involved with them. It just seemed an active development in being with them and doing the things which they enjoyed, which basically were the younger things in life – I went out with them, I did the things which they enjoyed. I joined in with them and I sort of came down to their age group and from there on in, just sort of drifted into this heavy petting. And that's all it was really. There was very little penetrative sex at all and most of the sex was more of comfort – comforting and soothing – from me to them. I never asked or required them to do it to me – sometimes they did, sometimes they wanted to, but it was never indicated that that's what I wanted.

Penetrative sex never took place until much later in the relationship, when they were getting older and that was usually indicated by them, that they wanted to try it. This is the crazy thing – it all seemed so natural. You know, when we had sex, afterwards it wasn't a matter of sort of, feeling dirty and running away and having a bath, or running after him in embarrassment – it wasn't; we just continued with the day or with the evening as it was and you know, it was all very nice. It was ... the only way I can put it – it felt very comfortable; we were comfortable with each other – there was no silent embarrassment on either side.

HARRY

For a long period Harry put clear limits on the kind of sexual contact that he would allow himself to make. It remained almost hidden from the boys themselves and his fantasy seems to be more important than the act itself. However when the circumstances were finally safe enough, the fantasy was realised.

I felt for my own sort of selfish designs that I wanted him there on his own, but at the same time he brought a couple of his friends with him who were interested in games and things like that, and it was nice to have their company. I mean, I got nothing sexual out of it, but it was nice to have their company. And I sort of entertained thoughts that, you know, on one occasion, one of them will come on his own and, you know, something might happen. It never did, but I sort of fantasised a lot about them during the daytime. I mean offences did take place, because although I didn't see it as sexual, they would sit on my lap. They would sit on my lap and, you know, I would stroke their leg and occasionally kiss them. So I mean, offences did take place, but not to the extent that I would have liked to have happened, you know, had there been just one of them there on his own.

I describe them as not sexual because they certainly didn't see them as sexual. I did, because I was sort of doing something with them that later in the day, when I was on my own, I would be thinking, 'Oh well, if they'd have been willing, then what would have happened after that would have involved us getting into bed or doing something together.' But as far as they were aware, I'm sure – the police interviewed ——, I saw his statement and his statement said categorically, 'No, nothing had ever happened.' And I mean, I'm sure from his point of view, nothing did. I mean, he probably thought I was a bit unusual in that, you know, I liked him to sit on my knee and I liked to sort of be close to him. He might have thought something, but I don't imagine his thoughts would have, sort of, gone as far as to say, 'Oh, we're having sex ...

can't have that.' I wouldn't have thought so, although by the time the police interviewed him, it was some years later and he was a lot older, so I'd be surprised if something didn't sort of question ... the question didn't arise in the back of his mind about, 'Oh well, thinking back on it, yeah, he probably was trying it on.' But I'm sure at the time he didn't think anything.

In fact, that was ... I was very, very careful in that sense, because I feared that if I went too far, they would sort of think to themselves, 'Oh, I'm not going there again.' I felt that if I ... you know, it was all right touching their legs, stroking their legs, but if I went too far up on to the thigh, then they would think, 'Oh, that's wrong, I mustn't go there again.' So I was very careful not to sort of go beyond a certain point with them. And you know, they ... by their actions, they sort of indicated to me that what I was doing, they didn't find particularly surprising. I mean just sort of, you know, some wrestling or something like that. They took that I suppose as ...

I was charged with several offences against two boys, well against three actually, although the third was very much a red herring. And you know, I ... in a way, I got some satisfaction out of just having the children around me, if you understand me. I mean it wasn't enough, I wanted more, but I was realistic in my thoughts. I thought, 'Well, you know, if I try to get more then I'm gonna get myself arrested, or they're going to sort of run away, or they're going to do something.' And so at that stage, I was being in those terms realistic about how far I could go without sort of running ridiculous risks. And I thought in terms of working for some organisation, which I eventually did. And I worked with one of the social workers there and that involved picking children up from their homes. These were children who had problems, difficulties at home, and it was a sort of relief for the parents to take the children out for an afternoon or sometimes back to the Children's Home. And there would be various entertainments for them, roller-skating or sometimes swimming, things like that.

And so, again, offences did take place, because I mean, they would sit on my lap in the minibus and things like that. And I would touch them, but they again wouldn't, I don't think, be aware. Again, one of the boys that I wasn't charged with, the police interviewed and he said in his statement, that, 'No, he never. I sat on his lap and he touched my leg, but nothing else', which was actually, absolutely correct, because, I mean, I did touch his leg but that's as far as it went, because I was afraid that if I did any more than that he would say something and you know, I'd be in a lot of trouble ...

... That's when the abuse really started, because from the very first night ... I mean, I had a double bed and there was also a foam mattress, it was no more than that. And when we went to bed, when we were getting ready for bed, I said, 'Do you mind sleeping with me in the double bed?' 'No, no that's great.' So I never even put the mattress out and we just fell into bed together and slept together, right from the very first night.

VERNON

The following extract is particularly interesting because of its description of the actual moment of seduction in terms of the abuser being seduced, and an absence of harm.

Well, it was then getting on towards the end of August and there wasn't much time left before the new term started. So I spent a few days throwing some stuff into my car and I went and collected him. And he had an older brother, and I said, 'Okay, he can come as well.' I took them off to a campsite in ——. We had two tents – one was a double, one was a single – and my plan was that he and his brother would have the double and I'd have the single. But when it came round to sleeping that night, the brother – who I didn't know at all, I'd only met him once before – put on a fit of temper and refused point blank to sleep with his brother. He hated his brother and wouldn't even sleep with him, so I said, 'All right, don't worry, you have the small tent and I'll sleep with him'. So, it was a double bag and we slept together and there was no sex or anything like that. We just slept together, you see. The next day we spent on the beach. We came back in the evening and when it got round to bedtime, I went off somewhere, I think it was probably just to the toilet or something like that. Anyway, I left this lad to get undressed and get into bed.

When I got back to the tent, he was standing there naked in the tent and he said to me, 'How do you do sex?', you see. I don't know what I said. I thought I said, 'Get into bed, you're cold', or something. And I thought to myself, 'Well, this is a question that every 13-year-old wants to ask, you know.' And I thought, 'Well, why not, what harm is it going to do?' So we lay there together there and talked about sex. He said, 'How d'you do it? How d'you do it?' I showed him and so we had sex. And I thought that was the end of it.

And then a week or two later, he came, as he had been doing, to stay at my house for the weekend and he wanted sex again and I thought, 'Well, in for a penny, in for a pound.' And after that, we had sex fairly regularly and it went on until he was 23 years old and he got booked. And ... well I admit, I enjoyed the relationship. There was – as far as I was concerned – there was no abuse. I never did anything that he didn't want.

DAFYDD

In this frank account Dafydd shows how he fulfilled his fantasies and relied on his victim's reputation protecting him. Having raped her, he ends the relationship and also ends his protection. In the second account Ronnie minimises through blaming the victim and delineating a hierarchy of sexual activity.

I got very close to ——. She accepted it. And she actually, outright came to say, 'I fancy you, you know. You're a really nice guy.' I got her to the position where she trusted me implicitly and consummated the relationship. Intercourse took place. I went to sleep on her. I felt really sick, you know, about that.

I knew that she was already a victim and I still went ahead ... in the face, taking my fantasies to reality, overcoming any resistance. The things I was telling myself – she won't tell; nobody would believe her because she's a known liar – a troublemaker; she's had it before, it's not going to hurt her. You know, actually putting into place where we could go. And the ideal place was – after hours – the boys' club; at the youth club, the youth centre – it was comfortable, quiet, locked the doors, great. Sit in there and do what we wanted.

And on the last time – took her back to the club and we had intercourse. I raped her. And on the way back, I stopped the car and said, 'Look, we can't go on love, I'm sorry, I can't see you any more.' And there was a very dramatic scene. The end product was, 'You fucking bastard, you dump me now and I'll fucking screw you.' And she did.

RONNIE

The offences were fondling and cases of mutual masturbation. There was one case – with the one I mentioned to you, the one that lasted a long, long time – there was one case of oral sex with him, which I mentioned, came as a charge ... He had instigated that. That doesn't make it right, but I wouldn't have done it myself, because I didn't know ... do anything like that. But for the record, there was nothing like buggery, or intercourse, or anything of that sort.

JAMES

The core programme helped James to face up to the reality of his abuse. The programme uncovered what he'd always known, but had been unable to admit.

I saw a job advertised, so I applied and got the job. For about the first six months, year, my behaviour towards the kids didn't change; it was still inappropriate, without being criminal. But after that there was an occasion with one of the boys – he was very upset, there were a lot of problems at home, Dad had split; he was apparently very violent – and he got a letter and I happened to be on sleep-ins you see. And he came to me and he was very, very upset and I read the letter and I took advantage of the situation. And it just escalated from there, until eventually the children actually mentioned it to another member of staff – what was happening – and that's how it all came out. But I think, looking back now, I think a lot of my life ... I think a lot stems from what happened myself when I was 11. I think that was the planting of the seed, you could say, and it was just a question of time really, before it grew.

In fact, I even put it to one of the kids once, because I'd abused, slightly abused this one child who I was very close with, whom I formed a relationship with when he was actually in my unit, the younger children. And we'd been messing about like, fighting, and I had touched where I shouldn't have touched the child. And I was in his room and I remember him coming up to the door and he wanted to talk, he wanted obviously, because I actually got round to saying, 'I'm really sorry about what's happened; I'm going to go and hand in my resignation.'

Now at the time I thought I was trying to stop myself, but I was really saying, 'If you say anything it's going to make ... I'll only lose my job.' And I was putting that added burden on him, to get rid of this guilt from myself. And I got the expected reaction, 'Oh no, no, no, as long as it never happens again, you can't.'

It's taken the core programme to make – this may sound a little bit arrogant, but I don't think it taught me anything – but it got me to face what I already knew; buried it young, I'd shoved it down and it really got me to face up to it. Because even in the court, I mean I pleaded not guilty and even in the court, I was more or less admitting, I was saying, 'Yes, I used to go to the boys' rooms late at night, talk to them, things like that, but ... ' So I was sort of, you know, I was nearly there, but I couldn't quite go that final step to say, 'Yes, you know, so I put them through all the horrible thing of giving up their natural privilege, you know.' Even on a video link it's ...

Physical abuse ... I mean, I would behave inappropriately by hanging around showers or the bathroom – things like that, you know – I would get kicks from that as well.

Minimising/Ambivalence About Harm

KIM

This short extract reveals how even in the face of an emotion as strong as hate Kim finds it difficult to link his abuse with any harm.

You know, I still have difficulty in coming to terms with the harm that I've done. For instance, one of the guys who I was with was married and he'd been a partner of mine since he was about 12 and he was 25. He 'phoned me up before I was arrested and asked me to come round; and the only reason he 'phoned me up was to come round to his house and have sex. And we did. We went to bed and had a smashing time. And two days later the balloon went up, I suppose, and his name came out of the bag. And in his statement he said, you know, that he hated me. Now I'm thinking, 'Why did he hate me? Did he hate me for what I'd done, or because he was exposed?' Which was the most probable? I'm not sure. I don't know. And I don't suppose I shall ever really find out, which is rather a shame.

RONNIE

Ronnie, on the other hand, is struggling to understand why the realisation of the harm he was causing came only after he had offended. The extract also provides an interesting example of how the granting of permission can survive moral scruples.

And as you appreciate, I suppose when things come to light you are forced to think. And I was being forced to think for the first time, basically, and that's hard to believe. I mean, I'm sure people are not going to believe that because they'll say, 'You're a professional. You know better. You should have thought about these things before. You should have thought about if you were hurting these children.' It's a terrible thing to say that I didn't, but it's true. It's not naivety, I mean I'm not thick. I don't know, it's one of those things I still haven't worked out in my mind. Was it that the lust inside me was so great I was blocking out reality? Or was I honestly thinking that I wasn't doing any harm? Was it a kind of showing love that went too far? I don't know. I'm still very, very, very badly mixed up about this, absolutely.

I know now I'll never be able to put this right. I mean it isn't like you've broken a window. You can go and mend the window and it's been put right. If I've hurt these people – the more that I think about it, the more I'm told about it, I have hurt these people – I'll never be able to put it right. Never. I don't know what to do. I don't know how I'll face it. I just don't know.

I still ask myself why I did it. Is it because I was evil? That's the first thing you ask. I never wanted to hurt anybody in my life. If I am evil, I hadn't planned to be evil. I obviously had feelings. I was getting something out of this, regardless of the poor victim. Because I'd told myself, not in words, but obviously I told myself it was all right. It didn't even dawn on me that I should stop. I don't know. I do have one or two regrets now. The other person I've spoken to in quite some detail about this – similar to the way I've spoken to you – is my family doctor, who is female.

My one dreadful regret is that I hadn't gone to her earlier. I couldn't have gone to my previous doctor, because he'd been my doctor ever since I'd been a child, right up until about eight years ago. I couldn't have gone to him, even though had I gone, he'd have been fine. She said that had I gone to her earlier, perhaps she would have looked for help for me. I wish I had gone earlier.

I can tell you what made me feel that it was something not right. It was one of those Esther Rantzen-type programmes. And I remember the time, the first time in my life, thinking, 'What you're doing is not right.' Not that it was terribly, terribly wrong, but it wasn't right. And I did think, 'Right, I've got to stop.' I didn't think I was harming the children, it just wasn't right. And something came up – and I'm not saying it was one of Esther Rantzen's programmes – a programme, that's all I can say, that people should go and talk to their family doctor; that's the type of thought. Could I go and talk to Doctor ——? But of course I didn't. I didn't go anyway until ... There was a long ... There was quite a long period when I know I didn't offend and I did stop – if that's the right word – and yet, within the last two years, I started again.

I've talked to people since my arrest. I've talked to my solicitor, the psychiatrist, and had a short talk to the probation officer here. Yes I've got to accept it. I know now, yes. I know I've hurt them. I don't know to what degree though. That's the point, you see. I don't know to what degree. As yet, I can't come to terms with that, from my own point of view. Will I ever come to terms with that? Because I worry terribly. There's nothing I can do any more to help those children.

JAMES

James vividly spells out the complex tangle of emotions surrounding his abuse and how he dealt with it by distorted thinking – conceptualising himself and his actions as different and therefore distanced from the reality of what he was doing.

I was in control. To a certain degree I suppose I was. In a horrible sort of way I think I was in control then. I think, in fact I don't think, I know, having worked with and studied children. We had to do certain courses which dealt with child abuse. But I always managed to, 'Oh but I'm different', sort of thing, you know. I knew that deep down ... but I just wouldn't face it. I was saying to myself, 'I am not harming these kids. These kids keep wanting to come up to me, every time I, you know, come back from being off-duty, they're all around me. How can I be damaging them? They wouldn't be behaving like this.'
    Typical child abuser's warped mentality. And yet deep down ... because, quite often, once I had committed abuse, I would go into my room and just literally break down in tears and think, 'What the cowing hell have you done now?' And a couple of times I very nearly said something to my Head of Care, but cowardice I suppose keeps you back. And I would ... Every time I'd abuse the children, I would say, 'Never again, that's it', you know, 'This has got to stop.'

Fantasy

HARRY

And these were lads that I was very fond of and again nothing sexual happened. They didn't at that stage, come to ... I only sort of met them off the premises. And going to the cubs, obviously there were always other people around. But you know, I did sort of fantasise about them when I got home. You'd think, you know, it would be nice if they would come to the house. And in the case of one of them, eventually, it did come to pass that he came up to where I was living.

Reaction to Exposure

DAFYDD

Dafydd illustrates the trauma of arrest with his thoughts of suicide and the desperation which leads him to subject his victim to further pain in court.

And they arrested me and took me away and I just completely blanked out – everything; not knowing anything about it. And I was put in custody for a week, then remanded on conditional bail back to my family. And I thought, quite seriously, on two occasions about suicide. And in the end some younger people that knew her heard through the police, 'Oh, Dafydd won't be back here any more.' They said I had resigned from the youth centre for various reasons. 'He won't be back any more – he's had a spot of bother.' And they said, 'Is it because of what —— said?' 'Yes. Why?' 'Oh, she told us last week she was lying to get him into trouble.' The policeman, all credit to him, got in touch with my solicitor and said that he ought to interview these two kids, might help me out a bit. In actual fact, in the Crown Court ... I regret very much now, not having the guts, the strength, the moral strength, to actually stand up and say, 'Hey, don't take this to court. I'm guilty.'

No, I was clutching at straws all the way through. I'll regret that 'til the day I die. The whole four-day, three-day period of that week where I brought everything to a head, was one where I was committing suicide myself.

RONNIE

Ronnie, on the other hand, decided to keep his victims out of court. He concentrates more on the community reaction and his change of status from respected member of that community to sex offender. He alludes to the effect that the disturbance of the status quo had on the people who knew him.

May I say, when I was committed nobody had any idea. That's why when it came to light, as you will appreciate, it caused trauma. That's the only word you can use for it. I understand that, you see. I was away from it. Once you're arrested, you're not in that community and because I was living, as I say, 17 miles away. I've heard one or two things. There was a tremendous trauma amongst people who were nearest to me. Of the people concerned, none of them ever came forward, you see, with any complaint.

There was one person who left the area and, apparently, there was a programme on the radio and at the end of the programme he was asked if anything like that happened to him. And at first he apparently said 'no', but then he did mention it and that's how it came to light. The way it came to light from a police point of view, was completely different. When this came to light, they were in searching my home, as you appreciate. They took away diaries and in these diaries I'd mentioned people. I hadn't mentioned anything sexually explicit, or anything of that sort, but I'd mentioned people and it was obvious from things that I'd said over the years in the diaries that these people meant a lot. And then, needless to say, they started to go and question these people. Their response was interesting, in the sense that at first they didn't want to speak to the police. With pressure and everything, two of them then made statements. Two people I was very close to indeed made statements. And once it had got to that stage I saw his statement and I was determined that nobody would go to court. I made a complete list of everybody I was involved with. All these were given ... I gave them all to the police.

Apparently, some of these people were interviewed then. They're married. These were married people with children. Some of them were not very pleased that I'd made these statements. I may have done this in the sense that the police promised that in no way would these people be involved, no way that their families have to be concerned. Because I said, I'm not going to make any statement which would destroy their lives even further. It ended up then that nobody had to be called to court. It was a little bit one-sided. I wasn't happy; I had to face that. The person who made the original complaint – and I did read through his depositions – had things in there which were completely untrue. But it made no difference really, you were pleading guilty to the charges I told you all about etc.

JAMES

The struggle to be honest with himself was the main issue for James.

Oh, very difficult. And half of me wanted to sort of put my arms around them and say, you know, 'I'm sorry and I shouldn't have', you know. And the other half sort of trying to shut that all back down – 'No, they're making it up.'

Even then, I still wouldn't admit even to myself, let alone to anybody else, exactly what they were saying, you know. Ninety per cent of it was true. But I still couldn't even admit that to myself. Perhaps in my quieter moments, you know, when I'm lying in bed at night and someone will come in and talk about it, then you can, but even then you're still not ... You admit what's happened, but you're making the excuses. Well they were coming to me. They were saying you know, come on, come on, come on, come on. So you ... you're warping that and you're turning that into, 'Come up and abuse me.'

Masculinity

The theme of masculinity clearly threads through all of the extracts in this book, but it is usually there by implication and under the surface of what is being said. The following two extracts are rare examples of the offenders making the links between their abusing and their identities as men. In doing this, they present their own images of themselves as men, within the context of the macho cultures within which they grew up. The link with issues of power and dominance, expressed as they are inside the macho environment of a prison, are abundantly clear.

DAFYDD

I'd ruined everything. One of the main things ... not being able ... I can't drink, so I won't go out and get drunk and solve it that way ... Half a pint of malt and I'm anyone's. I suppose people think they can go out and have a drink and, you know, get rid of some stress and tension that way. Not me, though. Yeah. It's this macho image. I've been brought up with a macho image. Yeah. All my uncles – from my earliest recollections – all my uncles were miners. Wow! You know. Talk about hard men. And all my boys, all my cousins, all hard men. Yeah. It's the way you look after your own problems, you know? ... Traumatic. Lost everything. Well I haven't lost everything. I've thrown everything away.

DAVID

I think, through the core programme, I'm looking at my, you know, what they call the 'cycle of offending'. I think that what I identified within myself and my past were contributory factors, through my making a choice to offend. It's my choice in the end, not the factors, I decided. But lots of people have been brought up in the same situation ... I think it was the need ... I can identify the need to fulfil an image, a macho image and a role which I could no longer do. I mean, with the stress and the strain of maintaining that image, it was finally giving in. I think the need to find some sort of 'love' or emotional outlet and contact, which I hadn't got, which I'd suppressed all those years; and my chosen profession multiplied that suppression.

And if it makes sense, I'm glad now that it didn't develop further, because I would have hurt somebody else ... I must take on board that I could well have. There's a sort of positive to that, as well as the negative. Perhaps if it had developed; perhaps I wouldn't have gone down the other track. But there I see how I developed into David the abuser and suddenly I think all the pent-up envy as a kid, of the older brother – older uncles come abusive brothers – came into the fantasy. The fact that the macho image, male culture, everything, I think, contributed then to this fantasy world of opting out to something which I could fulfil; and with all the dangers and the fears, which yes, frightened you, but also excited you in a perverse way.

Work Environment and Collusion

DAVID

David explains in intricate detail how he used collusion within his profession to empower himself as an abuser. What he describes is not simply a process of colleagues giving him permission; rather he exploited their complicity and reluctance to challenge, in the manner in which he disclosed pieces of information and by selecting to whom he disclosed.

I think the fact that the relationship I had built with a young lady had gone disastrously wrong, because in the end I chose it to go disastrously wrong, but chose to blame the system, the job, the family; all these things which were pressures in my life. And also a huge element was in the sense of there were people within my own profession who gave me permission to offend. By, again, my knowing intellectually that they were offending, or knowing of their offending behaviour. I'm almost intellectualising too, 'Well if they can get away with it, so can I.' Sounds awful now. Something which I abhor now.

I think, in the sort of stage when one's gaining permission to offend, one knocks down one's ideas of, 'It's wrong, it'll hurt, this abuse.' I think as an abuser, or at that point a potential abuser, I think you make yourself aware, or sensitised to those who you think are involved in this sort of thing – who are possibly abusing – through rumour, through gossip, through this sort of thing. I wasn't conscious of doing it then, but now I'm very conscious of the fact that you go to a colleague for help, advice, and again with this consensual lie that you create for yourself as well as those you're abusing.

I think you choose those you go to, who'll give you the advice you want rather than the advice you need. And so I think, that's where I looked to colleagues who I knew – subliminally, or quite openly – would give me the answers I wanted, or wouldn't say, 'Hey, this is wrong.' And so that's what I mean in that sort of idea. I've no evidence other than just speculation that they would be involved in an abusive situation, because if I had evidence now, I'd have no scruples at all about saying, 'This person is an abuser and should be stopped, because he's creating victims like me now.'

I'm much more aware now of the damage I've done and the damage others could be doing. But you can't do that by just suspicion. It's very difficult to do that. When I was arrested, I felt that I had to ... I spoke to the authorities about certain persons who I felt were a danger and things were followed up from there. But again, it frightened me. I go back to that fear thing; that you don't choose those you know are going to stop you; you don't choose those that are going to help you in a positive way. If you think you are right, you choose somebody who's going to help you in a positive way for wrong. And I think, well I know, looking back now that I chose people who I knew wouldn't stop me in my tracks, basically. And it goes ... the 'what if' syndrome inside – which I pushed past – what if I'd chosen somebody who'd said basically, 'Stop, look at the damage you're going to cause to the victims, to family, to your friends, to the situation, to yourself. Feel sad now – feel bad.'

Instead, I chose somebody who I'd seen in the company of young males and put two and two together in my own mind. I went to them and I said, 'You know, you could get into trouble if you're not careful.' Really, what I did was approach it from 'I'm not involved in this, but look you're involved, be careful, people will talk.' And the answers I got, 'Well, I wouldn't worry, people will talk anyway.' And you got all the stock answers, which I now know are answers of total denial about what they're doing. 'Oh, I'm not doing any harm. They wouldn't be here unless they wanted to be here', which is classic of course. 'I'm not doing anything wrong.' Therefore I took from those sort of answers, answers for myself, then, to go on and to abuse. 'Oh yeah, yeah. If it was doing any harm, if he didn't want to be here, he wouldn't be here. I'm not a ...' I think it just fuelled the lie I was creating for myself. So that's exactly how it happened. And I came away from that situation empowered to abuse, which is a frightening situation now. So it's not in any way shifting responsibility for my abusing on to that person. But there is a certain responsibility which they share that I went on from there.

Explanations

DAVID

In attempting to explain why he abused, David tries to unravel a complex web of needs; the need for company, the need to have people close and the need for physical contact. These, amongst others, are linked to his ability to relate more easily to young people – the theme of power lies under the surface.

I find it very difficult to draw the scheme of how I became an abuser, because I find it very hard not to slip into excuses, cognitive distortions about where I am. So that's why I find it very difficult to say, 'Well this happened, and that happened.' And you feel, 'Well, that's just an excuse', or whatever. I think it was very much to do with being isolated from friends, family, the whole system.

Having moved from a city situation, surrounded by friends, into a country situation; suddenly being on your own and actually craving company. I believe that the abuse developed through this craving company, and finding it so much easier to make company with youngsters, who are part of your world anyway, who relate to you. And then progressing that need for company into fulfilling other needs within yourself. The friendship and the trust that youngsters put in me. Upping their age, downing my age and then finding that I could satisfy other needs within myself – sexual gratification needs – by abusing. Thus developed David the abuser.

It's almost a progression of needs. Somehow the normal progression of needs wasn't fulfilled. Therefore it deviated off at a different tangent, which at the time was easier. That sounds a bit callous, but it was almost easier and required less emotional involvement, commitment and time, than if it had developed on a normal level. I think it was difficult to build relationships in the work I was doing. Well, I chose not to build relationships, the job didn't work for them in that there was lot of travelling, moving around. And suddenly, you're coming to a situation where you just feel a huge desire to have people close to you. But you also feel a huge need not to become attached to them, because you couldn't fulfil what was required from the relationship. I found myself in a sort of Catch 22 situation. I wanted company, but I couldn't put my part of the investment into that company. I wanted physical contact, emotional contact. I'd got some needs for myself, selfish needs which weren't getting fulfilled properly and so I found myself looking to wrong areas, illegal areas and a fantasy life developed around that. And I think that's where I was. David the abuser coming forward would mean that the fantasy life suddenly deviated. Not suddenly. I pushed it towards an area where it could be fulfilled, if you understand that thinking.

I had access to material that could fulfil my fantasy, whereas normal fantasy fulfilment was harder and more difficult and everything seemed to mediate against my fulfilling myself. I abused first of all when I was 29. And that came after a good relationship, where I built up relations with a young lady. And, yet again, everything seemed to mediate against that; the fact that she was in ——, and I was here. She got a job in ——. I was away. It was as though everything suited me to take the easy option and not make that commitment to a long-term relationship.

7 IMPACT OF THE PROGRAMME

The core and extended treatment programme for sex offenders, through which some of the men interviewed have passed, emerged as part of the Prison Service Strategy document of 1991. Depending on the length of their sentence, men are offered either the short core programme or the extended version. The stage at which this occurs within their sentence depends on a number of factors, and there has been criticism that in the case of longer-term prisoners, treatment comes too early in the sentence (Sampson, 1994).

Both treatment programmes draw heavily on the work of Finkelhor, in so far as they aim to challenge distorted beliefs and enhance awareness about the effects of abuse on victims; encourage abusers to take responsibility for their offending; and help them to develop relapse prevention strategies. The latter requires, first, that they identify the nature of their offence patterns or cycles; second, that they learn how to avoid high-risk situations. The extended programme, which is designed for longer-term prisoners, involves more specialist work and a more individualised focus.

In the interview extracts that follow, the men reflect on their experiences of the programme, and also on what they think organisations need to do in order to safeguard future potential victims.

KIM

The first extract reveals a very mixed response to the effects of the programme. Kim has been through two core programmes but is still unconvinced about having caused damage to his victims. In fact, he does not see what he did to his victims as abuse and has developed his own particular definition. However, he still sees the course as valuable and feels that it has contributed significantly towards his commitment not to reoffend.

I feel, on the therapy, that we're getting one side of the picture, really. We're getting the book side. What other people think of the damage that we have done – bearing in mind that these people have been publicly exposed for what has happened and that is obviously most embarrassing for everybody. And yeah, I can understand people being cross about that. I can also understand them being cross that my support has been withdrawn. I am there no longer. And I was a huge pillar of strength to a lot of these people. They used to phone me up, write to me expressing their problems at the time. And I used the best place I could to try and help them, guide them, sort them out. Very rarely by material things. I didn't buy them expensive presents or anything like that. No form of bribery at all. When I took them out, you know, it was really to enlighten them on a better side of life. I used to take them out into the countryside. I showed them what makes things tick out in the real world, took them swimming, fishing, walking.

The therapy has shown me how I can avoid further implication. I have now done two core programmes, and I've got an ongoing one to start as soon as I get out. When I've finished that one, I shall then go on to an offenders' course which I think is a monthly thing; it's like an alcoholics anonymous type thing, which is ongoing *ad infinitum*, apparently. To be perfectly honest, I'm still not yet fully convinced of the mental and physical damage that I've done to my victims; that hasn't really convinced me.

The victim awareness section of the course showed us a couple of videos relating to a daughter, or a step-daughter, who was abused over a long period – and I do mean abused. It certainly wasn't comparable to the type of activity that I've been carrying on with. I couldn't remotely relate it to that. I didn't see my children – my boys – as being abused at all. They came to me quite willingly, and the sex developed quite openly and willingly. There was no force, coercion, stress or anything to go with it at all. I didn't threaten to take away their goodies if they didn't comply. And if they ever said, 'I don't want this any more', right, it stopped and the friendship continued. And a lot of them did.

It went on like that. So I'm still not yet fully convinced that what I have done was devastating. I'm devastated at the thought, the possibility, and I'm also devastated that these people have had their private lives opened up to private scrutiny. That is bad. Just those points alone have convinced me that this will not occur again, and I've made positive steps to ensure that that will not happen. But they are the reasons for me not to offend again, not that I know that I have damaged people. The interesting course would be for someone to talk to these people now, after this long time. I don't mean the police or social workers; I mean an independent; person, just to talk to these people and find out what their true feelings are now. That would be interesting. I would like to know the answers, though. I would.

The core programme has done a great deal for me, apart from the sexual side, you know. It's how many people can come to the sort of fourth change in their life, basically. I left school and I did ... I've been through ..., so now I'm into a new realm of life. How many people can sit back for four years and have professional help to have a look at their lifestyle of the past and set up a lifestyle of the future? It's not many people have that opportunity, and I've taken full advantage of it. With my wife and family, I have counselling as well and we'll all do counselling together when we're out of here. So we've set up the basis of a whole new life – one without this therapy. So – yeah, the therapy has been worth its weight in gold quite honestly, because there are years of my life, you know, that did need looking at.

Coming into prison has been quite an education. I said this to various people and it sounds very strange; it's an experience I wouldn't have missed for the world in a lot of senses, really. It's good to have a break – to withdraw from life in general. I led a very fast life out there, at about 120 miles an hour – going all the time, very fast. And I didn't ever have time to sort of sit back and have a look, but now I've had that opportunity. I've also met an awful lot of people from all walks of life and found out what makes them tick, and relating to these people has been quite an exercise. It's also given my wife an opportunity of taking more responsibility in the home.

DAFYDD

The depth of the impact of the confrontational aspects of the programme is vividly described in the following extract. Dafydd expresses a considerable amount of guilt and appears to have internalised and accepted the degree of damage caused not just to the immediate victim, but to all the secondary victims as well.

The core programme actually forced me to look at myself and think all sorts of really bad things about myself, you know. I know there's good in here.

I think, devious bastard, how could you, knowing that she was a victim in the first place and then to compound that? It made me – it was a very emotional time for me. In fact, one of the other lads actually came into my cell and I – there was a point where it wouldn't have taken much for me to have got sheets up on the window. I was really distraught, saw myself for what I've done and it hurt, like, what I was looking at in the mirror and I couldn't see any way out.

And again, the ... I've only been emotional really, two times. Once was in prison, when Mr —— got the chink in the armour and wedged it open – prised it off; told him about when I was assaulted. And once, just before Christmas this year, last year, where, in my cell there, I just broke down completely. I could not stop crying. I was sobbing my .... I just didn't like what I was. I mean the reason it was noticed, because I got up in the middle of a church service and I just walked out. I just didn't feel worthy to be with anyone normal. And the vicar, he actually waved – signalled – to one of the boys to go and see if I was all right. And that was really a terrible, frightening time, when you actually see what you ... what you've done and what you've become through your own deviousness.

I mean, I've been told as well, that I put myself down a lot. But I think once you've put yourself down to a certain point, there's no further to go and you can start building yourself up. And what happens is, I've built myself up a bit and then I reflect again. People say that you've got to put your past behind you and live – look to the future.

My own thoughts on that is that I'm forgetting my victim. There's no empathy with the victim and I do empathise very much. I am told by people outside, that —— has settled down. She's got a family – and this is only four years ago – and that she's happy. That doesn't make me feel good at all, because she's always going to have that ... that she's been ... She has been wronged twice in her life – once by a family member, and once by a trusted friend. I'm always going to feel very ill, and I really do feel that I can't put that in the back of my mind and forget it. And I don't think anyone should that's harmed somebody. I don't think they should forget it. Ever.

And it's one of those things that for the rest of my life, I don't think I'll ever be able to forgive myself. They say that carrying guilt around is sort of damaging. To me it's a necessary part of paying your debt to your victim. Not to society, to your victim. Maybe I'm wrong in saying that. Maybe I'm wrong in thinking that way. I don't know, but to me it's not just one victim. I mean, it's ripples in the pond. It just keeps going out and out – ——'s a victim, ——'s a victim, ——'s a victim, my parents are victims, ——'s a victim, her parents and friends are victims, all my colleagues are victims, the whole community is a victim. It's just mind blowing.

JAMES

The impact of the directness of the approach adopted by the workers within the core programme is again evident in James's description of the early part of the course. He stresses the importance of the focus on his defences being dealt with first, thus making him more receptive to the victim's perspective later.

And I think, really, the first time I sat in the core programme and they said, you know, 'Let's start it, James', and it was just like a light inside of me that said, 'At long last you have a chance to really talk about what's gone wrong in your life and what you think of it and to sort yourself out, or at least to try and sort yourself out.' And from then on I could accept the blame, the damage I'd caused, everything. And ... nice – it's like somebody had picked a 20-ton weight off my shoulders.

I think what I needed was somebody to say, 'Look, stop your bullshit, because we know it's bullshit. Come on, just for your own sake, put the victims aside for a minute. Just for your own sake, admit what you've done and let's talk about it. Let's get it all out in the open.' I think if they'd have gone for the victim's perspective straight away I wouldn't have admitted it. But at long last, here was somebody who seemed genuinely interested and genuinely wanted to know what had gone wrong with me. And then of course, once you can accept, 'Yes, I've got this problem', then you can pick up the victims and say, 'Well, no, look at the problems you've dumped on these poor sods. You have put them in the position that you were in. It would be horrible, but in ten years time, we might be sitting here talking to one of the victims of your victims, who now you get to finally confront.' It needed computation for me; somebody just to say, 'No'. Because, of course, your parents, everybody, they know damn well you've done it, but they say, 'Don't worry James, we know you wouldn't have done these crimes.' Which of course is ... You go to the Magistrates' Court and the Crown Prosecution's solicitor stood up and said, 'Very minor offences', which of course is all just building your defences quite nicely, you know. He did do this, but he's just said, 'very minor'. What am I doing here, you know, if it's very minor? And that's just reinforcing your, you know, 'The bastards are trying to get me. The bastards are jealous of what I was achieving with the kids.' I was just rebuilding on that.

DAVID

For David, the relationship between himself and those around him, and his recognition of the need for others has been brought into focus by the experience of talking in depth about himself in the group. This seems to have been a profound process of coming to terms with himself, and challenging his reconstructed self.

Isolation. There's a sense of huge isolation in there. I've got to watch now. I realise it within myself. It's a bit silly, but as I said, I'm happy with myself and I force myself to relive now, to get me to make some friends. It isn't so easy to go to oneself.

I think what I have virtually learnt is that I want to be a social animal, whereas before I felt I was my own man. I could cope on my own. I didn't need anyone else. Now I realise that I do need other people. I need to be part of a group and share where I am with people. And I've found that one of the benefits of the core programme is the fact that I have related to people – my own peer group, really – and spoken deeply about me; who I am, what I am, what I've done; in ways I've never done in my life before. And that frightens me as well. To get to 41, 40 years of age and never having had the confidence to expose myself and be accepted. Because the one thing it has taught me is that for the first time I can weigh where I am, who I am, what I am and people still like me; whereas before, it was unacceptable, in both my work and my family; and I feel much more a rounded person, much more at ease. Whereas I'd describe myself in the past as diseased within myself; I'm much more at one with myself now, here. Happier.

I link that with the opportunity the core programme's provided in actually forcing me to look at my upbringing, my disciplines, my background – everything. Even in my work, you're taught to shut up and keep quiet about yourself and about others. So it's a completely alien experience. And yet, that alien experience has, I feel, reaped me more benefits as a person than anything I've ever done. And then again, it's so sad that it's taken so long. The officers here think I'm going round the bend when I say I have found my prison experience to be a very positive one. It has negatives, but I've found that some very positive things have come out of this as well – because of these opportunities which I have never had before.

Previously, I put myself into a situation where I wasn't myself. I wanted to do other things. I wanted to be part of something else and that's always been my problem from the very beginning. Whereas here in prison, there is a need within me to be part of it, to conform, to be part of it, of the show, of the crowd. But I've changed now to be able to say, 'I don't want to, it's not for me. Here I am. There is the culture. If it wants me, it can come and take things from me and I'll come and take things from it.' But now, I identify where I am and I identify who I am and what I am and I'm quite happy – if that's the right word – to be me now, for the first time in my life.

In my own experience and from listening to core groups, everybody plans their abusing meticulously. You've got to, otherwise you will get caught or it will not happen. And every abuser has to pre-plan where they're going and how they're going to achieve their aims, from their thinking, to their giving permission, creating opportunities to abuse. And you've got to do it to achieve your goal. But I say that and identify it from where I am now. Where I was then, I didn't recognise that I was planning these things out. You assume they're just happening, or you persuade yourself they're just happening. You're not aware of the analytical planning going into it at all. But when you do look back and review it through hindsight, you can really see.

What Could Help?

KIM

Whilst praising the quality of the programme Kim emphasises that motivation is the critical factor. For him, involvement has to be voluntary and he argues that the use, therefore, of the parole system to manipulate people into cooperation is counter-productive. He sees this as undermining the value of the course and encouraging dishonesty and game playing.

Therapy is very good, providing it's not forced on you. If therapy is the only option that you have of getting out, you'll do it. If you're forced into therapy in that way, you can play one off against the other and you can come through therapy, if you're articulate enough, with a whole pack of lies and run everybody round in circles. It'll do you no good. You'll say the right things in the right places. Everybody has a beautiful painted picture of you and you'll go out no better off than when you started. And I've seen that happen without a shadow of doubt, because what we talk about back on the wings has got nothing to do with what we talk about in therapy.

Some people are very, very well aware of what they talk about in the therapy. It can be taken down and used in evidence against you, basically. And there's a lot of those guys that have got crimes all locked in the cupboard. They're still there undiscovered and they're staying there. And if they were to open up, to really open up in therapy, you know, they'd have a whole string of other offences. So they keep it very well locked up – all sorts of feelings that are still locked away. And if they think they can get away with it, they will, unless they come here on a voluntary basis – and it's got to be really voluntary.

The system they've got at the moment whereby you do therapy or you don't get parole, it's a carrot that dangles in front of another carrot. Parole itself is a huge carrot and it's a diabolical system that causes so much stress it's unbelievable. But the therapy on top of that is another carrot that you've got to take before you look at the next carrot – it's not on. And as I say, people will abuse the system and do. A sex offender's life is hell, really. We're the best con-merchants in the world. There's no doubt about that. But you can't con a con-man and they can talk their way through most therapy groups if they want. That's where the voluntary bit's got to come in. You can only get a bloke to open up his heart if he wants to change his lifestyle. If he doesn't want to, you won't and no therapy in the world will change him.

They aren't going to change that, I don't think. The therapy itself is good. The core programme is a good programme. If you want it to, it will certainly bring out the right bits and stop you dead in the tracks at the right places and make you have a good look at yourself. But as I say, it's totally pointless if you don't want to. Now I want to, because I've got a lot of things out there, and if I don't change my life I lose the lot. And that, basically, is the biggest incentive to make a change, not the content of the core programme. The core programme has helped me to do that. But if I hadn't got that impetus to start with, the desire to want to change, the core programme would be totally useless, totally. So to get the best out of everybody, you've got to show them what they've done is actually harm a child; that this is what you've done.

DAFYDD

Dafydd describes how confrontation had an adverse effect on him. Far from opening him up, it made him reluctant to talk and whilst he accepts that the approach might work for others, he believes that a focus on the positives would have been more helpful. He also says that follow-up is vital as part of a relapse-prevention strategy.

I think it's a conglomeration, or a build-up of ... I don't know ... I think of many things. And it's difficult to home in on one, without making it sound like I'm trying to justify or make excuses. I mean I had that on the core programme, where I was actually ... I was crying and I was told, 'I think you're talking a crock of shit.' That didn't endear me to open up any more. It shut me up completely. I just clammed up for the next half hour or so and just let him get on with it. They were slagging me off left, right and centre, you know. And I just thought, 'this is getting nobody anywhere at all'. And it wasn't until I came back from break that I actually composed myself enough to take the situation back to where I wanted it, you know, 'let's start again'. This wasn't doing anyone any good at all and rather than open me up, it just shut me up. I didn't feel that there was anything to be gained by that – it wasn't helping anyone. Certainly at that moment I needed help to get it out and I don't criticise that as such. I just think that everyone is different. They're used to it being run one way and it's silly, you know, to expect that all the time.

Everyone is very complex inside and I think you've got to deal with that – not tear it apart in case you're left with nothing – very slowly, just rebuilding the good side, those bits that I know for my own survival – for my family's survival, you want to get back out again.

As soon as possible after conviction the thing is to address the offence. Just over two years, two-and-a-half years, I've waited to come here on this core programme. And it was only when I kicked up because my mates that came here after me were on a core programme and I wasn't chosen. I started moaning, kicking up, shouting, saying, 'What the hell? I'm waiting to go on a core programme. There's people that have arrived here after me that have only been in a couple of months and they are going on a core programme.' I said, 'I've been in over two-and-a-half years, I want to go on a core programme.' 'Oh, all right.' And they found a spot. But it was only because I kicked up about it.

I think as soon as possible after the conviction you should be put straight on it. And then, after, to keep the relapse-prevention going, it only needs be one session a month, or something like that. Through my probation officer, I'm doing what they call the —— group with probation officers. I want that, but it's a year and I want that year, to go on the course. I think it's one evening a fortnight for a year – that's great. Virtually a carry-on from the core programme; it's relapse prevention, it's being honest with yourself. I think that anyone who's committed any offence against the person needs to look at himself, or herself very, very carefully and closely, motivation-wise, everything. I'm not a hurtful person, I don't see any need for anybody to hurt somebody. I'm not that mad. It doesn't lay easy with me.

RONNIE

Ronnie hasn't as yet been on the programme, but has heard from others that it is worth while. However, he articulates a concern felt not just by other prisoners, but also by other commentators on the programme (e.g., Sampson, 1994), that the people running the programme are not sufficiently trained.

I don't think there's any help that can be given, to be honest with you. This is kind of something I've got to live with. It's easy in here at the moment, because I'm able to put it to the back of my mind. That's the easiest thing to do with all problems isn't it? – put it to the back of your mind. Put two years' time away from you. Live life to the full now and don't think about this – that's the easy way out. But I know eventually that I've got to come back to this all the time. I don't know whether I'll ever, ever, have any peace of mind again. Part of me thinks that I won't you see; it's one of those weird things. I think if anything will help me not to transgress again, it is this feeling that I will never be forgiven for the first batch. Therefore, there must never be any more. That's the feeling. If it's positive in that way, that's positive.

I don't think of the future at the moment. I've got two-and-a-half years ahead of me here. All my friends around me down there, to them, it's a sentence, it's an upset. To me it's a comfort.

Is it because I don't have to face reality for two years? In one way, but the core programme will help with that. So in a way, I'm hiding now. In a sense, I'm hiding here. I'm happy here. I've got the education programme which is something I really love doing. It's ridiculous to say that one should be happy and contented in prison, but yet I am. I'm happier now than I've been for a long, long time.

It's a retreat. What came into my mind the other night was that in my period in the 1950s – I was brought up in a cathedral city – some of the Sunday school teachers were the Anglican nuns and of course, they used to have retreats then. Young people went into retreats. I'm hiding the fact there're bars on those windows by pretending that this is a kind of retreat – and it is. And I haven't been so calm and contented for years. Now what I'm going to be like in two years' time, I don't know. I know I mustn't become institutionalised. I can see it and I can see it can happen. Something I'd have said beforehand, before coming here, 'I won't be like that', I can see how that can happen, because you don't have to think in this place. But that again is for the core programme. It's got to be essential, and it's got to make you face things, like I'm trying to do with you today. See, I couldn't stop talking. I needed to talk today. You coming here has helped me. It's ridiculous really. I'm supposed to be the one helping you.

What would help us is a difficult question. I've talked to a few very similar – when I say similar, I don't know what their crimes are but they've got problems similar to mine and they're going into the core programme, like myself, open-minded. We are a little bit worried about the core programme, in the sense that it's in the hands of ... I use the word amateurs, and that's not running them down. But we would be happier if the core programme had more professional people in charge of it. That's one feeling we've got. I suppose we do need to open up in one way to professional people. And we feel that professional people may be able to pick out our problems, to help us in the way well-meaning amateurs can't. This is a little thing that is bothering quite a few of us here. I talked to two people who've been through the core programme and both of them have come out of it positively. Both of them say they're glad they've been through it, and both of them have said – they're professional people, one is a teacher like myself – both of them have said that they're very, very glad they've done it, in the sense that they are seeing themselves properly perhaps, or in a different way, for the first time. This gave me reassurance. But the kind of overall fear we have about the core programme is whether it is in the right hands.

I think this is something we won't be able to say in the core programme, because these people are our officers. But this is a general feeling we've got here, so really we are possibly laying our future on the line in the core programme. Some of us, maybe, we're hoping for miracles, but if it can only help us in a way to get to terms with what we've done, to stop us offending again, then I think we can face the outside world in a safer way. If that's the right word. But I saw an officer last week and I asked about it. There's a waiting list for the core programme now. And I will get on it, because I did two things. I volunteered in the beginning and he said, 'That's good points for you.' If you've got people who are open-minded and want to do it, I think that's the kind of person they want as well. It would be interesting to talk to you after it was over. I may have a different picture.

DAVID

The effects of labelling and the generalising of the response to 'sex offenders' are seen by David as contrasting sharply with the positive experience of the core programme. This, together with the wish to be moved on after the programme to a non-offender culture, seems to be a plea to be recognised as someone who has changed.

Some of the negative experiences in prison I would think are its lack of ability to cope with an individual; its lack of any sense of enabling people to fulfil their potential; the lack of any concept that a man can have addressed his offending behaviour and be different. A sex offender in this place is a sex offender, is a sex offender for the rest of his life.

The fact that staff within the prison – some of the staff – some are I think notable exceptions, but their work is undermined by others, with the continual jibe of, 'Nonce', and things like that, which is a sort of prison word. The positive sides I would say, are opportunities to share with people at a deeper level because you are forced into a new culture. Some of the positives are that you make some exceptionally good friends, who you feel you'd like to relate to on the outside, as well as inside. Some of the positives are that you can have opportunities to have the time to think and assess and see where you are going.

And one major positive for me has been the core programme here and what that has given me – benefits, I hope, for the future.

I think it's a great mistake that you are kept here after the core programme. I think once you complete the core programme you should move on, because there's an awful sense of lack of motivation. There's a sense that you're back into a world of those who perhaps are not prepared to adjust their offending behaviour. And I find it increasingly difficult to cope with those people now. It sounds like the pot calling the kettle black, but I find it increasingly difficult now to have sympathy or empathise with anyone whose offending behaviour is not addressed. I have no sympathy at all for those people. If they're not prepared to do that, then they're just perpetuating what the negatives are of this place – that sex offenders always carry on, which is sad.

Prevention

JAMES

In exploring how he might have been prevented from abusing James reveals work situations in which there was a lack of support, a culture inimical to revealing problems, an ignoring of overt signs of abuse, a lack of police checks and a completely unmonitored system for providing references.

I think really what I was – if I can go back to when I was, you know ... I had very, very ... The Head there, he was brilliant. He was so human too. He would stay off. He would not be involved with any of the particular years. He would just float. The only time he ever came inside the union was if there were absentees. For most of the time he was just close and his deputies – there was always one of them – would watch, obviously, when you're dealing with kids. They would always support you, but you might be called into the office afterwards and he'd say, 'You made a right bloody balls of that, didn't you?' But they'd talk about it, you know, you wouldn't just get the rap over the knuckles. You would talk about it. And also, if you handled a situation well, they'd also pull you into the office and say, 'That was bloody well done. You handled that really well, you know – great.' And that sort of thing is important. If you had a problem, you could always go and talk to either of them, in fact a lot of the time they would say, 'Why don't you slip out for half an hour, 15 minutes – there's a pub just down the road, we'll buy you a pint and we'll talk about it.' The school I worked at after that ... the attitude was sort of, 'Well, if you can't stand the heat, get out of the kitchen.'

I mis-handled an incident. We caught two of the boys. They'd
slipped out of the dining room while I was supervising, obviously
smoking. Now they were very, very hard on smoking at the school.
It was horrible, get the Bible. I think at times there was room for a
more sensible attitude, particularly when their smoking harmed
no-one. But anyway we had to stick by the rules. When these kids
came up, they stank of cigarette smoke, so I took them down into
the union and I really ripped into these two. There was also a
selfish reason because, you know, by this time of the night. I was
late going off duty, so I wasn't particularly a happy chappy anyway.

And this one child who was very, very unbalanced, ran down
the union, smashed a mirror. First of all he was just making his
own protest. And I was just standing there and I was thinking,
'You're no threat to yourself, no threat to any other child, just get
it out of your system.' And when he saw that was the method I'd
decided to take, he went to cut a vein on himself. So I thought,
'Right'. I went to grab him; called another member of staff and the
other kid was there, and you couldn't let him stand there and the
boy was really going for it this time. I mean trying to cut his
throat. But at no time was he threatening us – it was all inward.

I eventually managed to get the glass off him, and got the
headmaster. I then left the situation. I thought, 'Well I'm the one
that's brought it on. All the time I'm standing here, he's still going
to be going on. Whereas if I get out of it now, we've got the glass
off him, he can't hurt himself, and if I get out of it he might calm
down.'

Now I wanted to talk about this, because I felt bloody awful,
you know. I'd just had a child try to commit suicide – and he had.
Towards the end he was serious. He was really trying to do himself
in. I knew it was not exactly my fault, but I'd exacerbated the
situation through my handling. I wanted to talk about it. I wanted
to talk about the threat, but nobody responded. I had to fill in the
official thing and that was it, as far as they were concerned. Nobody would sit down and talk it through with me. How should I
have done it, you know, what should I have? ... etc. And I just got
this feeling of inadequacy really. I felt really inadequate, you know,
because I'd ballsed it up. I could have bloody killed that child in a
way, through my insensitive handling of a very minor situation.

You know, I mean, even to talk about that, but they wouldn't. I
think that sort of support system is vital, because you're working
in a very, very pressured atmosphere and the way you feel with the
children is ever so important. And because we're only human beings, as you get tired, as you're coming towards the end of your

ten-day stint, you do get ratty, you do get short-tempered with the kids. So you need somebody there to say, 'Right, thank you James, I will deal with this now. You go and make the tea', or something like that, which neither of the two English institutes had. You know, there wasn't the support there amongst the staff.

Again I think ... somebody I could have talked to – really wonderful – and somebody the kids could have talked to, because ... the school which actually ... maybe I'd been out of it, but I think a lot of the children felt I was the only one that would listen to them. And I think that is one reason why so many of them did, sort of, gravitate towards me.

On a personal thing, I don't know, it's very difficult. A lot of times I'd have wished there had been somebody I could talk to while the abuse was going on and said exactly what was happening, not within the school, but maybe within the local authority, some sort of ... I don't know, probation or social work, or support. Somebody who for something ... even if I ... a couple of times I wanted to say, 'No, I shouldn't work with this child.'

I tried to get one boy taken out of the unit when it first started going from just looking to touching. I actually tried to get him off the unit. I mean, I could not see me telling them that it was because I fancied him. Now there should have been ... in a way that was a cry for help, I think to myself. I realised it was getting out of control; the urges were, you know. Looking was no longer enough, I felt I wanted to go further. And I think, you know, I don't think, I know, that was a clue for help for me, that I'd dropped a sort of, the line into the water to see if anything bit, but unfortunately they didn't.

At long last, if you liked somebody, it bit, you know. Because ages before it all came out I happened to be working for ——, and one of the boys I was abusing was sitting out the back, in his pyjamas, drawing and I'd just been down to the pool, you know, to see someone – naturally enough, so I could keep an eye on someone. And I came out to the ... and I went and sat out the back, because I'm not a talkish person. And he showed me the picture. So I leant over his shoulder and I said, 'Oh, nice one.' And I sat there and he said, 'Will you draw me a cartoon,' because I was not bad at whacking out cartoons. So I sat there and he sat himself on the left. But of course, I've moved him fully on the left and I'm sort of leaning over drawing ... and I saw the headmaster look. Now the headmaster never said anything to me, but on the Monday, the Head of Care called me in and said, 'I don't know quite how to put this James.' And I said, 'Well, usually the best way is –

just say it.' And he said, 'Well, the headmaster's asked that you would not touch up' – I think he said – 'not touch up the boys in the television room.' Now if he had those suspicions, then why the hell didn't he do something? You know, if he thought that I was touching up the child, surely an investigation should have happened then. You know, looking back on it now, there were warning signs there. The staff must have picked up on it.

I think if somebody had come up to me then and said, 'What the bloody hell's going on?', I'd probably be frightened there and then, which would have saved ... I'm not blaming them, you know. It's my fault, but we could have ... I'm pretty sure ... But I think you tend to ... either you don't think it, or if you do, think, 'No' and sort of push it to one side, don't you? Because it's a subject that you do not want to confront.

Proper training is needed. I don't mean the sort of ad hoc ways. I think you need people that have done – perhaps not the whole social work qualification – but have done some of it, in child care. You need payment – properly. You know, you are not going to get people that have done two or three years' college training to go and work in these sort of places for five, six, seven, eight thousand pounds a year, which is the sort of money that you are talking about. You know, even seniors are only earning ten or twelve thousand. I don't know what it is now. So you've got to train them properly and then you've got to be prepared to pay them properly.

You've got to get the right kind of person. Not just having Mrs Jones down the road, who's got a couple of evenings spare, because – without being nasty to those sort of people – it's just pocket money. You've got to have people coming in, but you mustn't get too involved – which is one of my problems – because I became too wrapped up. It became my life. But you've got to care. You can't just leave a child bawling his eyeballs out. You can't just walk in to watch and say, 'I'm sorry, it's ... I'm off duty now. It'll keep to the morning.' You cannot do that. You are just reinforcing that child's rejection. That's a very extreme example, but those sort of things happen, you know, 'tough, I'm off duty'. You've got to get better, higher calibre people. And also you have got to toughen up on people like myself getting back into the jobs. Because if you really want to, you can do it. They will argue against that, but it's been proved time and time and time again. At ——, in the two and a half years I was there we had never had a police check. Now that is bloody disgraceful. Because you know... there's two or three staff are like that, you know, two or three staff I know. I could write to —— and I could get a good reference.

So, we've got to train and we've got to pay. If you want good child care, you're going to have to pay for it.

VERNON

According to Vernon, instead of using the Criminal Justice System and the pointless deterrent of prison, the civil process should be brought into operation and victims provided with compensation.

What should happen is that for people in my situation it should be a civil case. They should be sued by people who feel themselves to have been wronged and if it's proven that wrong was done, then they should receive compensation. But I don't believe locking people up in prison does any good at all. Victims of a crime of passion, which is what all sexual crimes are, are not going to be killed and are not going to be robbed because everybody that commits such a crime knows that if they're caught they'll go to prison. They still do it. You cannot deter them if they're determined to do it, because they're in the grip of emotions which are too strong. And therefore, saying that prison is a deterrent is a nonsense – it isn't a deterrent.

All you can do is address the causes of the problem, which is a matter, I suppose, of counselling. But it seems to me that even that is ineffective when you get to my sort of age. If it had happened when I was in my teens, yeah. If somebody had said to me, 'Now look, you're a homosexual, you've got to face up to this. You're in a country where this is totally illegal and where you can do this, that, and the other.' Yeah, that would have been better than anything. But it's a bit late now – 25 years after the event – to say to me, 'You've got to go on therapy', or whatever.

I mean, the truth of the matter is I have no such illusions whatsoever. I think I'm well past the male menopause if there is such a thing. I just couldn't care less to have sex with children, women, old men, anybody, you know. My interests now are in gardening and art and computers and things like that. So if they want to waste their time giving me counselling, that's fine; I'll go along with it; doesn't worry me in the slightest, but it all seems so pathetic. And of course they never asked me in this place. They never asked me about these things at all – it's a take it or leave it situation. You are told to do this, so right, you do it, you see. They all feel that they are doing terribly important work. Frankly, I think that it's a great waste of time and if they were to ask their customers, they would realise this. But of course that would be putting their own jobs, their own status, on the line.

This business is a great deal more common than the public realises. I'm not going to tell you tales, but it goes on to a very large extent and a very large proportion of people in certain positions, like teaching and clergymen, scoutmasters – people like that, who come into contact with youngsters – I think a very high proportion are homosexual, although only a very small minority of them ever sexually assaulted a kid, or anything like that. And there's no way that will ever be stopped, unless they somehow offer an alternative. But I can't see what the alternative would be, frankly.

The only other thing I would say, is that people who turn to children for sexual satisfaction are, I think, very often people who find it very difficult to have any sort of relationship with adults. I think that's a general truth and that was true in my case, that I always found it much easier to get on with kids than with adults and this is why I enjoyed teaching so much; I could relate to them.

DAFYDD

The earlier theme of labelling, re-emerges in what Dafydd says about how the prison environment not only reinforces the sex offender label but also how the masculine culture induces inconsistencies between the messages of the programme and the behaviour of the officers. Attitudes which are challenged within the programme are exhibited by male prison officers towards their female colleagues.

I wouldn't know how to go about preventing something. I mean, I could only talk about my own case. Certainly better support for people that are out on a limb. Now with ... I think it's a new Criminal Justice Act, that if a vicar or a youth worker, or a social worker or whatever, hears of something, they are honour-bound, legally bound to report it now. That's good, 'cos when I ... on the quiet, phoned up the police – a very close friend, a social worker – I said that I had this case and that she was terrified of going to the police. He said, 'Dafydd, do all that you can to get her to report it herself, because we cannot take it second hand. We just can't, you know, it would fail straight away.' —— wouldn't, she was so frightened of her family's reaction and who could blame her? She would obviously have to go to court and tell everything, or there would be social workers climbing all over the place, who she would have to tell. And she knew that she had a reputation for being a bit of a fibber – people wouldn't believe her. Terrible dilemma she was in – talk about Catch 22.

I honestly don't really know how you can put blocks in. Certainly the law's moving in the right way, but there's been a flood – the flood-gates have opened now for complaints and that's got to be good, it's got to be good. There aren't enough core programme officers. There aren't enough core programmes being run, I don't think. This is my personal, you know. Here there are too many disruptions, in that, oh, officers have got to do night-duty even though they're core programme officers, so we'll cancel next week. And you can't do that. We've got to keep the momentum going. We've got to have regularity, so that you know where you are; you know your time's coming, or you know that somebody else's time's coming and you can help them with it, you know. And we were going instant and heart trouble time and you can't do that.

Again, personally I think – I've heard criticisms of this from other officers as well – they leave you down. They don't build you up and end on a high note, you know, just lift you that little bit. You need to be lifted sometimes. There are quite a few that were mental wrecks, really emotional wrecks for days after their time in the hot spot – what we call the hot seat, giving your actual account – just couldn't talk to them for days after. And they'd obviously been crying their eyes out, because they were red-eyed. And ... I don't see a lot of mileage to be gained by leaving people down. I see mileage to be gained by bringing them down, but then lifting them up and saying, 'Look, it's okay, never forget your victim, never forget what you've done, that's not the end of it – no, you've got to go on from here, you've got to rebuild.' You don't help him rebuild all that much. There's a lot of fine-sounding talk, but they don't want actions.

I'm not the only one, there're a lot of people who have heard officers talking about us behind our backs, or openly to other officers. And there are officers here and they go, 'You bloody beast', you know. 'You should be hung, Nonce', you know, which is prison slang for a sex offender. The chaplain also has noticed this and also some of the officers' actions towards their female colleagues in uniform. In a place like this, it's not on. They need to look at themselves very carefully, at the way they run their side of things, you know. They're telling us one thing in the core programme and they're doing exactly the opposite with their female colleagues – openly.

8 CONCLUSION

In the opening chapter of this book we made it clear that we were not putting forward the accounts of the men interviewed as representative, either of stories that might be told by any particular group of perpetrators of sexual abuse, or of any type of abuser–survivor relationship. The extracts add emphasis to that point: they are, for instance, spoken by men who, except for one, have abused young boys, whereas we know that the majority of survivors of abuse are female. It is, perhaps, our focus on men who abuse those in their care that accounts for the high number of male survivors in these accounts.

However, in their variety and complexity, the narratives do provide illustrations of particular components of a range of theoretical models. For example, there is a substantial amount of evidence within the descriptions concerning the perpetration of abuse of the four-stage process propounded by Finkelhor. But the transcripts do not in any sense constitute a test of that or any other theoretical model. Rather, their value lies in the detailed picture which they provide of the thoughts, feelings and motivations of individuals who have abused power to seek sexual gratification. The transcripts represent the stories of these particular men and, therefore, provide an understanding of their point of view which can be placed along-side understandings derived from other research based on larger samples.

So what the reader will have encountered in the last five chapters is the men themselves, as constructed through their own descriptions, explanations, justifications and excuses. The validity or truth of what they have said requires some discussion. However, before moving on to that, it is important to give some consideration to the process through which we as researchers went in order to establish a context conducive to the telling of stories. Moser and Kalton (1983) identify three conditions for the successful completion of survey interviews. They are conditions that it is possible to generalise to other interviews, and which may provide some explanation as to why the men in this study talked so freely and without apparent inhibition. The first condition is *accessibility*, or the degree to which the interviewee has access to the information sought. The second is *cognition*. This is the extent to which the interviewee understands what is required of her or him. The third condition is *motivation*, which in turn is conditional on how much the subjects of the interviews feel valued.

The men in this study talked very easily, fluently and openly with a minimal level of prompting from us as interviewers. We speculate that this was because the process of interviewing, in part at least, satisfied the three conditions distinguished by Moser and Kalton. Certainly the interviewees had access – in fact exclusive access, to the information sought, because the content was essentially their life stories; the narrative style of their responses is evidence of the fact that they understood what was required of them; and the amount of time that they devoted to the process suggests that they felt valued enough to talk for several hours into a tape recorder.

It is also appropriate to ponder how far the nature of the interviews, and our styles as interviewers, contributed positively to the process. We consciously adopted a non-directive and reflective style of interview and used what May (1993) describes as focused interviews. These are sometimes referred to as informal interviews. Their potential value lies in the fact that they create the opportunity for interviewees to develop their own agenda, express their central concerns and to talk relatively unconstrained by the structure of pre-determined questions. May argues convincingly that they allow people to talk within their own frame of reference and contribute to a more fundamental understanding of their view of the world. In this sense they allow for the challenging as well as the confirmation of official truths.

Inevitably the telling of stories involves reconstruction of past events and interpretations of their significance for the teller and others. Because they are reconstructions, such stories – as some of the extracts show – will reflect shifts in attitudes and thinking as well as distortions. Whether what is being said is the literal truth is perhaps unimportant. The stories do represent a version of the truth and, in so much as they do this, they challenge the accepted truths about men who commit sexual offences. Buckley (1995), in a discussion about the links between masculinity and offending, asks a highly pertinent question; namely, that if sex offenders are totally responsible for their behaviour, then why not shoplifters or burglars? Put another way, if it is legitimate within discourse on property offences, such as shoplifting and burglary, to focus on the contribution of socio-economic and political contexts to such offending, why not in discourse about sex offenders? It is as if sex offenders once identified, are brought into the treatment situation to be analysed and challenged entirely within the context of their individual decisions and actions. If nothing else, our study serves the purpose of placing such men and their offending within a context of social and cultural as well as psychological factors. Accordingly, if it is possible to place the accounts of the men interviewed within any one of the dominant theoretical models outlined in chapter 2, then the integrative model provides the closest fit.

A number of themes are discernible in the men's stories. In describing what we ourselves see in them, we hope to stimulate the reader into thinking about their own interpretations of the stories. In our view, the most pervasive theme of all the interviews is how the men conceive of themselves as males, and how they construct their own sense of masculine identity within both a personal and socio-political context. As Buckley (1995) suggests, the study of masculinity provides a framework within which to examine offending generally. We would argue that this must apply to those who commit sexual offences as well as the generality of people who offend. Therefore, it is important to place the stories of these men within an understanding of the heterosexual, white, male hegemony that dominates the social and professional settings within which their offending occurred. Wallis (1995) notes that the sexual abuse of children fits the abuse of power model, but that paradoxically the majority of perpetrators can conceptualise themselves as powerless and as failures as men. They see themselves within a hierarchy of power in which children are less powerful than themselves and, therefore, less threatening. Thus, their offending can be placed on a continuum which encompasses sexual satisfaction, the abuse of power, sexual subjugation and exploitation (Gocke, 1995). Moreover, men sexually abuse within a culture which maintains the ideal male role of dominance, and the acceptability of heterosexual relationships in which women are the subordinates and men the dominators. Perversely, sexual exploitation is trivialised and denied whilst at the same time men who commit sexual offences are demonised. Buckley (1995) identifies the prevailing themes of stifling emotion, achievement, aggression and sexual competence. She argues that masculinity becomes a set of precepts which if adhered to can be a further reward of being seen to be a man.

In their descriptions of their formative years, several of the men reveal their expectations of themselves as boys and how these were shaped by the construction of masculinity of those people near them. So Kim's lack of interest in football and cricket is defined as weakness, and this weakness is exploited through the bullying of his brother and his friends. In contrast to his 'macho' father, Kim labels himself as a softie who craves physical affection from a distant father. Vernon highlights the importance of not making a fuss when his foot is crushed by a horse, and equates that with the virtues of independence and self-reliance. Ronnie recalls listening to his father's violence towards his mother. It is also clear that Ronnie suffered considerable mental abuse from his father, and that this experience shaped his definition of harm. Ronnie hasn't behaved like his father and, therefore, has never hurt anybody. Stifling emotion and the pre-eminence of the physical over the intellectual occur again in David's account of being accepted by his peers and demonstrating his manly ability to suffer the physical abuse of his brothers in silence. Likewise Harry, who won the admiration of his peers by resisting pain, and then witnesses the sadistic and legitimised cruelty of a housemaster inflicting punishment.

Each of these illustrations are interesting in themselves. Yet their greater significance lies in what they say about how the men define abuse of power, and how such abuse is mirrored in the cultural spheres in which they grew up. Their label, 'sex offenders' should not serve to obfuscate the part played by those cultural spheres in shaping and sustaining attitudes that underpin permissions to abuse the vulnerable. Thus, for David, there are clear parallels between the street culture of his childhood – characterised as it was by hardness and suppression of emotions – and, perverse as it might seem, the culture of self-sufficiency and detachment (as described by him) of the Church.

It is interesting to reflect on this issue in relation to several of the men in this book who highlight their homosexuality, and elucidate their discomfort in male environments and within some of their relationships with men. At times in their descriptions they present their abuse of children as homosexual behaviour and, by implication, extricate it from the abuse of power model. Ironically, therefore, they are exploiting societal prejudice about gay men to place themselves outside the precepts defined by Buckley. Cowburn and Modi (1995) note that hegemony is both embodied and sustained in the various products of our culture that describe some identities as positive whilst denying others. The denial of a positive identity for gay men provides a convenient 'denial' for the abuser of young boys! Much discussion about the aetiology of sexual abuse is dominated by psychological explanations which are detached from the broader cultural context. This is discernable in the stories of the men who participated in the study. Invariably they seek psychologically defined explanations for their behaviour and its effects on their victims. In so doing, they isolate their offences both from the abuse of power model and the concept of harm. Glaser and Frosh (1988) argue convincingly that the definition of sexual abuse is not dependent on whether or not there is discernable harm. Yet we see in the extracts a burning curiosity about whether the victims enjoyed the sexual contact, or experienced it within a loving relationship, or whether they were harmed by it. It is as if positive answers to these questions will somehow legitimise the abuse. Our point is not that sex offenders will try to minimise or justify their offending – they are not alone in that, and it is a point repeatedly made in the literature – but rather, that a limited psychological discourse about sexual abuse runs the risk of fortifying those minimisations. More importantly, the eschewing of the cultural dimension from discussion sustains organisational environments in which abusers can operate unchallenged.

Finkelhor and Korbin (1988) make the point that sexual abuse that occurs in day care is like most other sexual abuse in that it involves adults using a combination of bribes, misrepresentations and threats to commit sexual acts with children that range from fondling to intercourse to oral–genital contact. However, they distinguish abuse in day care by reference to particular problems of management and control which are manifested in terms of location, timing, duration and frequency. We would add that abuse in such settings, be they school, church or youth club, is more likely to be unchallenged, ignored or colluded with if masculinity is not addressed as an issue. So if the men (and women) in those organisations do not understand the way in which their own definitions of masculinity influence and contribute to the culture of the organisation within which they work, they are less likely to be able to identify and respond to situations in which power is abused. David's, James's and Kim's descriptions of how they not only survived, but were supported in organisations, provide vivid illustrations of this point. The primary functions of care and protection were eroded not simply by the behaviour of the skilled lone manipulator, but by the conduciveness of the organisational culture to abuse of power. This point is also germane with regard to organisations involved in the treatment of men who have sexually abused. How can a treatment programme premised on the idea of reshaping men's thinking so that they do not abuse power function effectively in organisational environments characterised by white male and heterosexual hegemony? How can the treatment be effective if the approach used by programme leaders is confrontational and thereby mirrors the same version of masculinity in focus?

The men's accounts of how they abused in their work settings reveals how the way in which significant others view sexuality and masculinity impinges on supportive action and inaction. In Vernon's account, a male head teacher acted with callous unconcern for a distressed boy who had been bullied. Although there is no suggestion that he was knowingly abandoning this child to the clutches of an abuser, his actions had that effect. Moreover, those actions were possibly conditioned by views about manliness and male roles. In James's account, a male colleague actually observed what he defined as inappropriate behaviour – clear warning signs – but simply expressed concerns. We can speculate that such a response was constructed from a definition of a power hierarchy within which a potentially abusive colleague still came before a potentially abused child. And in David's account, colleague priests who might collude or even be abusers, were easily identified by the nature of their relationships with boys. Paradoxically, their visibility to an abuser priest was most probably directly dependent on their invisibility to others within the Church; and that invisibility was itself dependent on a failure to understand the manifestations of abusive power.

The theme of sexual identity dovetails that of masculinity in several of the men's stories. What is striking is the extent to which sexual development occurred within personal worlds placed in the shadows by disapproving parents and a wider society. Secret worlds provide little opportunity for the kind of norm testing that is necessary for the formulation of an identity that makes personal sense in a social context. Thus James, one of only two interviewed who talks about being abused himself as a child, is left in his formative years to ponder on what he describes as his 'warped sense of sexuality'; and Harry is deprived of sharing his love for another boy with his mother. The link with the secret world of sexual abuse is not necessarily causative, but the development of secrecy is nevertheless a useful learnt strategy for the future abuser.

The initial curiosity that stimulated our interest in this study centred on the potential link between the employment careers of men who abuse those in their care and the abusive career itself. It almost goes without saying that we did not expect to demonstrate such a link in this initial study with a small group of men. However, we did encourage the men to talk about their motivations in relation to employment and what emerged throws some interesting light on how work can provide an ideal environment for the abuser. The amount of convergence between career and abuse motivation varies from the explicit, to the implicit, to an apparent absence of any.

It is clearest in the case of Harry, who saw in voluntary work the opportunity to form relationships with children who could provide him with affection. From his description it would seem that there was no process of checking or vetting his background before giving him access to very vulnerable children. This occurred at a time when there was less public awareness of the extent of the problem. However, a recent case where a man convicted for sex offences gained access to young boys as a voluntary sports coach shows that vetting procedures do not always operate.

Harry openly acknowledges his dual motivation; it is there more by implication in the cases of Kim and James. Kim closely links the invitation to engage in voluntary work – again with no checks – and his awareness of the potential in the situation to abuse. Similarly, although he makes no connection himself, James very quickly offered to undertake other staff members' sleep-ins when he first took up employment in a children's home. The fact that he later reveals this tactic as part of his broader strategy to manipulate the system so that he could abuse the boys in his care strongly suggests a pre-determination to use his employment for that purpose. Such a connection is less obvious in the case of Dafydd who describes his motivation purely in terms of a desire to help youngsters through youth work. However, his later use of pornography as a blatant means of drawing young people into sexual activity does throw some doubt on the purity and integrity of his original intentions.

David, on the other hand, explicitly rules out any link between the processes of becoming a priest and an abuser. What is interesting about his narrative is his description of a sub-culture within the Church which not only contributed to a failure to identify and deal with the problem, but also provided him with 'permission' to engage in abusive behaviour. This appears to have been a revelation to him after he entered the Church, which lends credence to his denial of a link; he acknowledges, however, that he actively sought that permission through a subtle process of testing the water. The role of the organisation in the sustaining of sexual abuse is a theme to which we will return later in this conclusion.

Abuse of power is a strong and entirely predictable theme of the accounts of how the abuse was perpetrated: this fits exactly within

Finkelhor's theoretical model and the four stages of child sexual abuse outlined in Chapter 2. Each of the men reveal their motivation to abuse; vividly illustrate the process by which they removed their own inhibitors to abuse; describe in detail how they gained access to future victims; and delineate the manipulative and painstaking strategies which they employed to draw the children into exploitative relationships. Moreover, the descriptions of the relationships themselves are expressed exclusively in terms of adult to adult.

The men are not alone in their abuse of power because they recruit other adults into their action system, and on occasions other adults promote themselves. Thus a head teacher presents Kim with a 'problem child' who needs a father-figure: one powerful male hands over a vulnerable victim to another powerful male who fully exploits the fact that the child is from a less fortunate family and likely, therefore, to respond to the inducements that he has to offer. Another responsible male places an isolated child in the care of Harry who seeks the power of not just adult over child but adult over children with mental incapacity. Vernon and Ronnie exploit the power that teachers have over children, and Dafydd uses his victim's status as someone else's previous victim to exert control. How power is defined is crucial to the ability of each to grant themselves permission and to legitimise their actions. This is most graphically illustrated in David's definition, which itself is dependent upon a particular definition of masculinity. He explains honestly how he convinced himself that, because there was an absence of physical force or overt violence, what happened was consensual within an equal relationship.

The distorted belief systems reflected in the perverse interpretations of the status of relationships catalogued above permeate the descriptions of how the abuse was perpetrated. For some of the men the core programme has challenged these systems so that they are either clear about the degree of distortion – as in the cases of David and James, or still unaware – as in the case of Harry, or uncertain – as in the cases of Kim, Vernon and Ronnie.

Harry still relates his account of his abusive relationship with a ten-year-old boy as if it was a consensual love affair. In contrast, Ronnie describes all his relationships as caring ones. But he tellingly admits that, whilst he wanted to be a father to his victims, if he had been, he would have been a bad one. The notion that their victims had some responsibility for what happened – the classic trap within which abused children are placed by their abusers – is prevalent to a greater or lesser degree in all the accounts. Ronnie, for example, having accepted that he would have been a bad father, goes on to state that his victims made sexual remarks and made invitations to sex; Vernon denies that there was any abuse because he never did anything that his victim didn't want; and, Kim compares the 'real abuse' on the core programme video, which was coercive, with his own which he views as consensual. Such thinking, however, cannot be divorced from more general attitudes in society that women are somehow responsible for sexual assault and rape: attitudes ensconced in the judicial process.

The scale of the task facing those who run the core programme in prisons is exemplified by the illustrations of perverse thinking and interpretation referred to above. Appropriately enough, therefore, the programme – its impact and critique – is the final theme that we have identified as permeating the men's stories. There is no doubt that the programme has had an impact on those who have been through it. What is less certain, however, is the nature of that impact. While Kim still rationalises his behaviour as less abusive than the abuse shown on video, the programme has at least led him to contemplate the possibility that he might have harmed children. Perhaps more than any of the others, Kim illustrates the importance of follow-up work which is specifically focused on reinforcement. The capacity of the programme to have a discernibly real impact is highlighted most effectively by Dafydd who, although he was critical of some aspects of the programme, was made to look at himself honestly and to understand that his victims ranged far wider than the young girl he abused.

The subtlety involved in the learning processes triggered by the programme is well articulated by James and David who talked about the context of the learning. They both stress that it was essential that the deconstruction of self through self-challenge and reflection occurred within an environment of concern, appropriate help and acceptance. Without this, they argue, the opportunity for reshaping of identity would have been denied. In their analysis, they illuminate the intricacy and delicacy of the work involved and the high level of skill demanded of the group leaders. Sampson's (1994) concern about the non-professional status of prison officers who play a significant role in the delivery of the core programme is reiterated more explicitly than James and David by some of the other men.

A corollary issue raised by the men is the environment within which the training takes place. This relates specifically to the earlier discussion about masculinity, and the contribution of the organisational culture. There is clearly a question to be answered about the context in which the core programme operates. Can the programme, which is designed to challenge distorted belief systems and attitudes, be effective in a prison culture where men convicted of sex offences are labelled as beasts and nonces, and women are subjected routinely to overt sexism? It seems self-evident that the dominant male culture of the prison is an inappropriate place to challenge abuse of power; just as it is self-evident that criminal justice policy driven by macho politics is likely to fail to reduce male offending.

Other concerns expressed by the recipients of the programme relate to:

- the issue of voluntary or compulsory attendance, particularly against the backcloth of parole decisions; it is suggested that the link with parole undermines genuine motivation and encourages game playing;

- the predominance of confrontation as opposed to challenging, and the exclusion of a focus on positives;

- the lack of guaranteed re-enforcement or relapse-prevention strategies once the men have left prison.

In terms of prevention of abuse by men who through their statutory or voluntary employment have access to particularly vulnerable children, the men make a number of suggestions. First, steps should be taken to encourage a culture within organisations which is conducive to the revealing of problems. Some of the men in this study indicate that their pattern of behaviour might have been changed if they had been able to confide in someone that they could trust. Of course, the quality of this kind of prevention hinges crucially on the motivation of the would-be abuser, and research suggests that such motivation is likely to be low. Nevertheless, cultures that are inimical to the discussion of difficulties compound the problem, and changing those cultures can only improve the situation.

Second, there must be increased alertness to the obvious and less obvious signs of abuse. In their descriptions several of the men indicated that the evidence of what they were doing was there for people to see, but it was either ignored or missed. The key to this is training, which should focus on attitudes and understanding of sexuality as well as basic identification.

Third, systematic police checks are essential, coupled with the follow-up of references. Although the situation with regard to both has improved in recent years, questions remain about the tightness of procedures – particularly as far as the use of volunteers is concerned.

Finally, helplines for abusers should be set up. Such facilities now exist very appropriately for the survivors of abuse, but there are few specialist resources for perpetrators. Support and help is available after the event but not before. Not all abusers are amoral and, as the stories illustrate, guilt, remorse and the desire not to abuse are part of the complex web of emotions experienced by the prospective abuser. The idea that communicating the problem to a skilled and objective outsider might be preventative may not be as fanciful as it seems.

We began this book with a review of the subject area and, in particular, the predominant theoretical models of child sexual abuse. Whilst not necessarily representative, the stories provide a substantial amount of corroboration of the central tenets of those theories: abuse of power, distorted belief systems, institutionalised male power, low self-esteem, socio-cultural influence, and precondition. To that extent the stories provide confirmations rather than break new ground. However, what the detail and depth of the stories bring into sharp relief is, first, the capacity for honesty of a group of men who are generally treated as if they are pathologically dishonest; and, second, their normality. By this we mean that, in the generality of their lives, in their aspirations, their need for human contact and acceptance, their stories are unremarkable and could have been told by any group of men. They are members of society. They are sons and fathers, friends and colleagues. They are not outsiders, but unfortunately are treated as such when exposed as 'sex offenders'. They provide, therefore, a very convenient diversion away from the contribution that the rest of 'normal' humanity makes to an environment in which the vulnerable are exposed to the suffering of sexual abuse. The concept of 'abnormality' obscures rather than illuminates, and thus decreases the chances of prevention. We hope that these stories cast some light into the shadows.

REFERENCES

Adshead, G., Howett, M. and Mason, F. (1994), 'Women Who Sexually Abuse Children: The Undiscovered Country', *The Journal of Sexual Aggression*, 1:1, 45–56.

Baker, A. and Duncan, S. (1985), 'Child Sexual Abuse: A Study of Prevalence in Great Britain', *Child Abuse and Neglect*, 9, 457–67.

Bandura, A. (1965), *Principles of Behaviour Modification*, New York: Holt, Rinehart and Winston.

Banning, A. (1989), 'Mother–son Incest: Confronting a Prejudice', *Child Abuse and Neglect*, 13, 563–70.

Beckford, Jasmine (1985), *A Child in Trust*. The Report of the Panel of Inquiry into the Circumstances Surrounding the Death of Jasmine Beckford, London Borough of Brent.

Ben-Tovim, A., Elton, A., Hildebrand, J. Tranter, M. and Vizard, E. (eds) (1988), *Child Sexual Abuse Within the Family: Assessment and Treatment: the Work of the Great Ormond Street Team*, London: Wright.

Birchall, E. (1989), 'The Frequency of Child Abuse – What Do We Really Know?', in Stevenson, O. (ed.), *Child Abuse: Public Policy and Professional Practice*, Hemel Hempstead: Harvester Wheatsheaf.

Briggs, F. (1995), *From Victim to Offender: How Child Sexual Abuse Victims Become Offenders*, St. Leonards, Australia: Allen and Unwin.

Buckley, K. (1995), 'Masculinity, the Probation Services and the Causes of Offending Behaviour', in May, T. and Vass, A. (eds), *Working with Offenders*, London: Sage.

Butler-Sloss, Lady Justice, E. (1988), *Report of the Inquiry into Child Abuse in Cleveland 1987*, London: HMSO.

CIBA Foundation (1984), *Child Sexual Abuse Within the Family*, London: Tavistock.

Cleveland County Council (1988), *Report of the Inquiry into Child Abuse in Cleveland 1987*, DHSS, Cmnd 412, London, HMSO.

186 BETRAYAL OF TRUST

Colwell, Maria (1974), *Report of the Committee of Inquiry into the Care and Supervision of Provided in Relation to Maria Colwell*, London: HMSO.

Corby, B. (1993), *Child Abuse: Towards a Knowledge Base*, Buckingham: Open University Press.

Cowburn, M. and Modi, P. (1995), 'Justice in an Unjust Context; Implications for Working with Adult Male Sex Offenders', in Ward, D. and Lacey, M. (eds), *Probation Working for Justice*, London: Whiting and Birch.

Creighton, S. and Noyes, P. (1989), *Child Abuse Trends in England and Wales 1983–1987*, London: NSPCC.

Davis, G. and Leitenberg, H. (1987), 'Adolescent Sex Offenders', *Psychological Bulletin*, 101, 417–27.

Department of Health (1990), *Survey of Children and Young Persons on Child Protection Registers, Year Ending 31 March 1989, England*, London: HMSO.

Dobash, R.P., Carnie, J. and Waterhouse, L. (1993), in Waterhouse, L. (ed.), 'Child Sexual Abusers: Recognition and Response', in *Child Abuse and Child Abusers: Protection and Prevention*, London: Jessica Kingsley.

Dominelli, L. (1986), 'Father–daughter Incest; Patriarchy's Shameful Secret', *Critical Social Policy*, 16, 8–22.

Elliott, M. (1993), *Female Sexual Abuse of Children: The Ultimate Taboo*, Harlow: Longman.

Finkelhor, D. (1984), *Child Sexual Abuse: New Theory and Research*, New York: Free Press.

Finkelhor, D. and associates (eds) (1986), *A Sourcebook on Child Sexual Abuse*, Newbury Park, CA.: Sage.

Finkelhor, D., Hotaling, G., Lewis, I. and Smith, C. (1990), 'Sexual Abuse in a National Survey of Adult Men and Women; Prevalence Characteristics and Risk Factors', *Child Abuse and Neglect*, 14, 19–29.

Finkelhor, D. and Korbin, J. (1988), 'Child Abuse as an International Issue', *Child Abuse and Neglect*, 12, 3–23.

Finkelhor, D., Meyer Williams, L. and Burns, N. (1988), *Nursery Crimes: Sexual Abuse in Day Care*, Newbury Park, CA.: Sage.

Ghate, D. and Spencer, L. (1995), *The Prevalence of Child Sexual Abuse in Britain: A Feasibility Study for a Large-scale National Survey of the General Population*, London: HMSO.

Giddens, A. (1989), *Sociology*, Cambridge: Polity Press.

Glaser, D. and Frosh, S. (1988), *Child Sexual Abuse*, Basingstoke: Macmillan.

Gocke, B. (1995), 'Working with People Who have Committed

Sexual Offences', in Williams, B. (ed.), *Probation Values*, London: Ventura Press.

Halsey, A.H. (1988), *British Social Trends Since 1900: A Guide to the Changing Structure of Britain*, Basingstoke: Macmillan.

Hendrick, H. (1994), *Child Welfare: England, 1872–1989*, London: Routledge.

Howitt, D. (1995), *Paedophiles and Sexual Offences Against Children*, Chichester: Wiley.

Johnson, T. (1988), 'Child Perpetrators: Children Who Molest Other Children: Preliminary Findings', *Child Abuse and Neglect*, 12, 219–29.

Johnson, T. (1989), 'Female Child Perpetrators: Children who Molest Other Children', *Child Abuse and Neglect*, 24, 3, 943–51.

Krug, R. (1989), 'Adult Male Report of Childhood Sexual Abuse by Mothers: Case Descriptions, Motivations and Long-term Consequences', *Child Abuse and Neglect*, 13, 111–19.

La Fontaine (1988), *Child Sexual Abuse: An ESRC Research Briefing*, London, Economic and Social Research Council.

La Fontaine, J. (1990), *Child Sexual Abuse*, Cambridge: Polity Press.

Macleod, M. and Saraga, E. (1988), 'Challenging the Orthodoxy: Towards a Feminist Theory and Practice', *Feminist Review*, 28, 15–55.

Marshall, W. and Barbaree, H. (1990), 'An Integrated Theory of the Etiology of Sexual Offending', in Marshall, W., Laws, D. and Barbaree, H. (1990), *Handbook of Sexual Assault*, London: Plenum Press.

May, T. (1993), *Social Research: Issues, Methods and Process*, Buckingham: Open University Press.

Moser, C. and Kalton, G. (1983), *Survey Methods in Social Investigation*, London: Heinemann.

Nash, C. and West, D. (1985), 'Sexual Molestation of Young Girls', in West, D. (ed.), *Sexual Victimisation*, Aldershot: Gower.

Parton, N. (1985), *The Politics of Child Abuse*, Basingstoke: Macmillan.

Parton, N. (1991), *Governing the Family: Child Care, Child Protection and the State*, Basingstoke: Macmillan.

Plummer, K. (1983), *Documents of Life: An Introduction to the Literature of a Humanistic Method*, London: Allen and Unwin.

Rush, F. (1980), *The Best Kept Secret*, Englewood Cliffs, N.J.: Prentice-Hall.

Russell, D.E.H. (1984), *Sexual Exploitation: Rape, Child Sexual Abuse and Workplace Harassment*, California: Sage.

Sampson, A. (1994), *Acts of Abuse: Sex Offenders and the Criminal Justice System*, London: Routledge.

Siradjian, J. (1996), *Women Who Sexually Abuse Children*, Wiley.

Spring, J. (1987), *Cry hard and Swim: The Story of an Incest Survivor*, London: Virago.

Wallis, K.M. (1995), 'Perspectives on Offenders', in Briggs, F. (1995), *From Victim to Offender: How Child Sexual Abuse Victims Become Offenders*, St Leonards, Australia: Allen and Unwin.

Waterhouse, L., Dobash, R.P. and Carnie, J. (1994), *Child Sexual Abusers*, The Scottish Office Central Research Unit.

INDEX

adolescent abusers, 27
Adshead, G. 26, 27

Baker, A., 14, 28
Bandura, A., 17
Banning, A., 26
Barbaree, H., 18, 19
Ben-Tovim, A., 26
Birchall, E., 2, 14, 15
Briggs, F., 3, 28
Buckley, K., 175, 176
Butler-Sloss, E., 12

Children Act, 3
child sexual abuse
    definition of, 2, 8–12
    incidence of, 2
    gender, 2, 14–15, 23–4
    history, 2
    employment, 3–4
    law, 9–11
    age of consent, 10
    consent, 10–11
    harm, 11–12
    extent of, 12–15
    incidence studies, 12–13
    prevalence studies, 12–13
    types of perpetrator, 14–15
    family, 28–9
    alcohol/drug abuse, 30
    organisational culture,
        151–3, 177, 178–9, 180
    employment career, link
        with, 179–80

CIBA Foundation, 2
Cleveland Inquiry, 3, 12
Corby, B., 3, 15, 17, 22, 23, 29,
    30
Cowburn, M., 177
Creighton, S., 28, 29

Department of Health statistics,
    24
Dobash, R.P., 27, 28
Dominelli, L., 16
Duncan, S., 14, 28

Elliot, M., 17, 26

female abusers, 26–7
Finkelhor, D., 2, 3, 9, 10, 11,
    13, 14, 17, 18, 19, 20, 24,
    25, 26, 28, 29, 30, 31, 178
Frosh, S., 12

Ghate, D., 13
Giddens, A., 2
Glaser, D., 12, 178
Gocke, B., 176

Hendrick, H., 3
Home Office,
    categories of offences, 9
Howitt, D., 3, 26, 27, 31, 32,
    33

Jasmine Beckford Inquiry, 3
Johnson, T., 28